Managing Strategically - 101 Creative Tips is easy to read and has breadth and depth. Each section should be carefully read and re-read, and the reader should evaluate how it pertains to a particular situation. More than 101 creative tips as the title implies. ...This is an excellent "how to" book for both novice and seasoned managers. Unlike theoretical management books, **Managing Strategically - 101 Creative Tips** contains a wealth of information that only one who has "been there" can convey. It is well written and organized and should be on every manager's desk.

Jim Gullickson
Manufacturing Manager

Mr. Tobin has developed a recipe for successfully conducting business by combining experience-proven techniques with a commitment to people. I highly recommend this reading for employees at all levels of an organization.

Brian E. Farley
Corporate Manufacturing Engineer
NEC America, Inc.

The book is light with great depth and a lot of meat.

Berry Serota
Pharmaceutical Sales

I have read it all and enjoyed it. ... a great sense of humor...

Dr. Kent Collings
Retired Dean, School of Business
University of Portland

After reading many books on management theories, **Managing Strategically - 101 Creative Tips** is a dose of reality.

Jan Kraxberger
Product Manager, Corporate Planning
Sequent Computer Systems

Great reading, great book. Congratulations.

Dan Poynter
Author of "The Self-Publishing Manual"

In reading **Managing Strategically - 101 Creative Tips**, I identified with many of the scenarios and found reinforcement in my own management beliefs and style. I believe this book will be beneficial for managers of every level, as it identifies everyday problems and offers sensible, practical, and proven solutions.

Karen K. Maddox,
Vice President
AmWest Savings Association

MANAGING STRATEGICALLY

101 Creative Tips

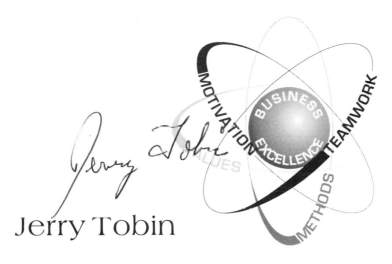

Jerry Tobin

A Practical Collection of Concepts, Models, and Strategies
for
Effective Management in any Workplace

Carrot/Stick Press
Hillsboro, Oregon

ISBN 0-9636424-1-3

Library of Congress Card Catalog No. 93-94000

Typography and production:
Meredith L. Bliss

Cover design:
John E. Hanan II
ICON Presentations
74 Wheatherstone Ct.
Lake Oswego, OR 97035

Illustrations:
Angie Tobin

Printed in the United States of America

Carrot/Stick Press
2373 N.W. 185th, #303
Hillsboro, OR 97124

PREFACE

This collection of concepts, principles, and anecdotes has been compiled at the request of several peers and previous employees whose thoughts have been improved, corrupted, or otherwise altered (depending on who is asked) through exposure to them. It was expected to be about a five-page piece, but it snowballed with time and additional requests from others. If this compilation causes some readers to be better managers, citizens, or coworkers, then it is successful. If not, perhaps at least some pleasure can be provided to most readers.

As a new manager in electronics manufacturing, I had the distinct advantage of working alongside approximately a dozen very good managers who held a healthy respect for each other and accepted a newling as part of their team without reservations. These other managers had mastered the fundamentals of management during their many years of combined experience and excellent company seminars. On the other hand, I was a true novice attending evening classes to learn the fundamentals with the hope of launching a long and satisfying new career. One particularly enlightening event was researching a paper on management of scientists and engineers which was later used for my own efforts managing manufacturing engineering groups. I have also been blessed to have later worked for and with many other excellent managers. This set of anecdotes and models is part of the legacy from this pleasant beginning and the subsequent pleasant years in management.

For ease of use, the material contained in the chapters is in alphabetical order for the first significant word in the topic name (for example, "the" doesn't count). The only exceptions to this are Chapter 1, the first four topics in Chapter 4 (*Decision-Making and Differences of Opinion*), and the last topic in Chapter 5 (*Twenty Important Effects Which Are Not Commonly Understood*). Also, because many of the topics overlap or refer to others, a complete index of the topics is provided after the Epilogue. This index follows the alphabetical order convention, identifies the page on which each topic is addressed, and enables the reader to use this text as a reference material.

In summary, the reader will immediately realize that some of the material in this book is unorthodox and/or comical, but that is because managers need to be able to relax and laugh as much as everyone else. However, the concepts presented are actually pertinent at some time or other in every workplace. Hopefully, this material will shorten the learning time for many new managers and refresh some veteran managers in their approaches. The information provided is not all common knowledge, but it has been compiled to share with anyone who can use it and to encourage everyone in a leadership role to think strategically to achieve both short-term and long-term results.

TABLE OF CONTENTS

Chapter I

Maximum Performance Can Only Be Obtained Through Motivation and Integrity

Though each manager needs to provide results as an individual contributor, the most significant measure of a manager's success is through results provided by his or her employee base. Consequently, each manager must possess the ability to motivate others to provide their best performance. Many managers consider this to be automatic or a direct result of applying position power. However, in the modern workplace, position power is a secondary motivator which should only be used in very rare instances. Instead, managers need to rely on logic, business needs, and persuasion to effectively motivate employees. In order for persuasion to be effective, the manager must inspire strong personal allegiance and be someone who is trusted by others. Several topics follow which can enhance a manager's effectiveness if applied correctly and with the right intent.

Extending Trust

The most important factor for successful leadership and motivating others is trust, and the only way this trust can be established is by extending it and watching to see if it is warranted. Some managers ascribe to a belief that trust should be extended only to those who are known to be worthy of it. However, this belief is a contradiction in itself because it precludes development of new trust. Admittedly, extending trust to the wrong parties can be expected to be disappointing and therefore constitutes a risk. But the ability to take risk is necessary for leadership, and the risk can be minimized through the use of the definition of "expect" and the application of good judgment. (Note: It has often been said that the only way to develop good judgment is through the exercise of bad.)

Honoring Promises and Integrity

Because of the need for a manager to have the complete trust and admiration of others, he or she must carefully keep track of promises offered and be known as someone who can be counted on to honor promises. Clearly, some events can occur which prevent delivery of something promised, but good managers will use sufficient caution to have these be truly rare and will find a way to provide a suitable contingency when these situations do occur. It must be fully understood by the manager that failure to honor promises is much more consequential than might be thought because this removes the ability to inspire allegiance or motivate employees through future promises. This is a major deficiency in some managers, often because of an aristocratic posture in which the manager in question projects a perceived personal superiority which exempts him or her from accountability to subordinates. (In reality, accountability to subordinates is every bit as important as to superiors because subordinates are the source of the manager's primary results. Without them, there would be no role for the manager to play except individual performer.)

Regarding integrity, a manager's word must be his or her bond upon which the employee can count faithfully. This is definitely not universally understood – *but should be*. If a manager cannot give his or her word and have it accepted, then that manager's only available motivator is the use of position power (thus always presenting the undesirable win-lose strategy). Managers must also realize that evaluations of past performance cannot retroactively change, especially for the worse. This latter is a practice which is employed by some managers who lack integrity or want to avoid providing earned rewards for reasons which are not performance-related, and they usually try to convince themselves that the changes are justified by new and better data. This and similar practices undermine the manager's credibility and ability to motivate his or her employees. (See *Management Practices to Avoid (Chapter 6)*.)

In fact, total integrity is absolutely mandatory for managers. Understandably, the manager may optimistically (and in good faith) oversubscribe sometime (See *The Alligator-mouth Syndrome*). And when this does happen through honest error, the manager should be allowed to have made a mistake (See *Allowing Others to Make Mistakes*) and receive continued allegiance and support.

Go The Extra Mile Yourself

For motivating people to provide extra effort or accept additional responsibility, one of the most effective methods is to set an example by doing these things yourself. In the workplace, managers can be observed who will assign tight deadlines and then relax themselves. Later, they wonder why the assignees don't exhibit the desired level of commitment to the task. Managers who exhibit high commitment can expect to have much better success getting the same from employees.

I first confirmed this watching a petty officer on a submarine assigned a crew to clean an area which was very difficult to reach because of numerous closely-spaced pipes and valves. At first, his crew contended that the area *couldn't* be cleaned well. Refuting this, he assigned himself the worst section, rolled up his sleeves, and began contorting himself to make even the least accessible regions examples of cleanliness. Laying on his back in oily water while the boat pitched and rolled, he showed his crew how to clean such an area properly, removing any suspicion that he would assign any task to them which he was unwilling to do himself or which actually couldn't be accomplished. Afterward, he discussed how to clean the rest of the area with them and helped them get started the next time they were assigned cleanup. The earlier extreme action was only necessary once, but his crew members were lauded several times later by their shipmates for keeping this previously filthy area so clean. In fact, when a new crew member would contend that the job couldn't be done, the others would quickly tell him not to let the petty officer hear this and would show him how to do it themselves. This was possibly the highest compliment because they clearly understood that when the need existed, the petty officer would go the extra mile himself and respected him for it.

In another situation, a manager suddenly needed to travel across two states (and three mountain ranges) on a day when a major snowstorm was expected within hours. The manager felt a commitment not to leave his assigned projects and their teams without scheduling two important meetings, delegating responsibility, and completing some important paperwork for a deadline. One of his previous subordinates, with whom he had strong rapport, knew that he was risking being caught in the snowstorm and asked him if it was okay for her to ask him something. Receiving his agreement, she asked, "What are you doing here still? Are you stupid or what?" While the questions might seem to have been sarcastic or disrespectful, the subordinate was actually acknowledging that the manager was going the extra mile himself. Laughing, the manager responded, "Yes, I'm that brand of stupid. And not only that, I've watched your work ethic, and in the same circumstances, you would be too." She agreed and he then told her that one aspect of being a committed employee is that you often put yourself last but that, as a manager and leader, you need to sustain this and to always set an example of doing what it takes to do the job. (See *The Curse of Duty*.)

The pitfall that accompanies this effect is the very real (and frequent) occurrence in which managers expect employees to have as much commitment as their own, even if it definitely exceeds the norm. Not all employees will possess the zeal of a dedicated manager, and trying to obtain this is unreasonable. Also, the manager who tries to always exhibit extraordinary commitment for the sake of setting the example is risking operating with diminished personal efficiency because of fatigue and not spending creative quiet time to properly attend to future business, home life, and hobbies. (See *Putting Your Job Ahead of Your Career* and *Personal Sanity and General Well-Being: A Model of Balance*.)

Pay for Performance and Performance for Pay

"Pay for performance" is a phrase often given lip service by managers who lack in-depth understanding of its value in increasing and sustaining improved business performance. While at first glance this phrase seems to refer to salary or base pay rates only, it actually can be easily extended to have widespread implications for formal and informal rewards. Frequent positive reinforcement for good results provides strong incentive to continue to provide results and gives the employee an understanding of what results are actually wanted. The reinforcement can be as large as a raise or bonus or can be in the form of a public statement, a meal, or even something as small as a soft drink at an unscheduled break. However, it needs to be something which the *employee* values in order to be effective (See *The Paid Trip*.)

The obvious corollary to "pay for performance" is performance for pay. This means that significant positive rewards should not be provided for weak performance – instead, employers have an inherent right to expect each and every employee to earn their pay according to current industry standards for their respective jobs. If the industry standard changes somehow, the employer can rightfully expect the employee to adapt to the standard. (For example, modern engineers and scientists can justifiably be expected to be able to use or learn a number of computer software programs which did not exist only a few years ago.)

"Satisfactory" Performance Is Not Good Enough

Each manager will encounter at least one employee with the ability to be a star performer but who is performing in the "acceptable" or "satisfactory" range. While the employee could continue to so perform with job security in most organizations, the manager actually has an obligation to both the company and the employee to call for a higher level of performance. Otherwise, the weaker performers will drag down the company profitability without being held up by the more capable employees, and everyone's job can be jeopardized. Ignoring this doomsday scenario, one must consider that to allow an employee never to earn the rewards which he or she is capable of obtaining is not necessarily being "nice" to the employee in question. Instead, such allowance may actually be mean. The rewards may be in terms of money, position, job satisfaction, self-esteem, etc. In any event, expecting employees to perform up to their capability falls within the bounds of rightful management prerogative and can be a powerful tool when used and reinforced properly. (See *Defining "Expect"* and *Pay for Performance and Performance for Pay*).

The Manager as Publicist

The American Management Association has allegedly, at least earlier, defined management as "getting work done through others." Consistent with this, the best managers motivate, inspire, and lead their employees to provide better results than they otherwise would. But many managers don't realize that their ability to get the best from their employees on a sustained basis is inseparably tied to the manager's loyalty to the employees. One of the best methods for a manager to demonstrate this loyalty is to serve as a publicist for the achievements of the employees. Whenever the employees provide extraordinary effort or results, the manager actually has an obligation to publicly acknowledge this, and most managers are both glad and proud to do so.

Managers also should publicize their employees' capabilities and accomplishments in private or small-group conversations with other managers and should actively seek opportunities to further the employees' careers. Each employee who receives benefit of a manager-publicist is a potential powerful ally, and publicizing deserving employees is also a slightly disguised declaration by the manager that he or she also has succeeded. (See *Shared Credit – Shared Blame.*)

The Messenger Role

Serving in this role is a significant need to be an effective manager. In particular, this role exemplifies complete objectivity. Employees will often refer to being given a raise, promotion, bonus, or disciplinary action by their manager, and too often they are correct. However, objective managers define performance standards ahead of appraisal events and apply these standards objectively so that all rewards (positive and negative) are earned and expected by the employee. In essence, the objective manager who stands behind defined performance expectations will not "give" any rewards but will instead deliver whatever is due, much like an unbiased messenger delivers the news – whatever it is.

Many managers never even seriously consider this role, much less achieve it.

The antithesis to this principle is *Management Through Negative Surprise.*

Motivation Through Compacts

Many employees seek career growth or higher rewards, and many managers stifle some such employees to retain their veterans or just fail to seize the opportunity to fashion a win-win situation. Instead, good managers help employees develop a strategy by which the employee can achieve his or her objective through added capability or improved performance. Normal results of this include better business results, higher employee satisfaction, and an enhanced ability to attract the best employees for future openings.

As an example, an employee wanted desperately to be promoted as an assembler but had a low efficiency rate. The employee and the manager negotiated an agreement such that the employee could be promoted if she could sustain specific performance levels for three consecutive months on an objectively measured combination of productivity (measured against published standards), quality (determined by an inspection error rate), and attendance in the workplace. Calculations showed that the particular performance levels provided sufficient profitability to offset the accompanying pay increase. When the data showed that the terms had been met, the employee was promoted. (See *The Messenger Role* and *Honoring Promises*). This employee shared her delight with her peers, and the next time the manager made a similar compact, the other employee was not about to fail to meet the expectations because of being so certain of the opportunity to attain the goal and be rewarded too.

The Paid Trip

I first became aware of this concept while researching the paper on management of scientists and engineers. In particular, one very thorough study addressed the ranked desirability of particular rewards for completion of a noteworthy project or task. Disagreement was evident between the desirability of two proposed rewards, a paid trip or a cash bonus. The author had sociological research data available by which the respondents could be compared for several personal attributes, and the split in the rankings of these two potential rewards correlated mainly to the creativity of the respondents. In particular, noncreative respondents ranked receipt of a paid trip (with a set itinerary) very high, but creative respondents preferred a cash bonus. (Perhaps they would rather plan their own trips.)

The importance of this information is much more general than the specific case of a trip vs. a bonus. Rather, it is demonstrative of two particular effects – the importance of providing appropriate rewards and a clear strategic error which often results in loss of the very employees who the employer most wants to retain. (Note: the same research showed that the most significant difference between employees who leave and those who stay lies in rewards and status.) Most managers dole out rewards which they themselves select with no participation by the employees. In situations where creativity is not an important factor, this strategy is viable, but in a situation calling for innovation, this will encourage the less-valued noncreative employee to "nest in" and drive the more-valued creative employee to the competition. This is a form of designed long-term failure for the company.

Defining "Expect"

In the usual sense, managers tend to use the word "expect" to stipulate a requirement with implied negative consequences if the expectation is not met. While this can be effective when dealing with those few people who respond most strongly to negative incentives, it will alienate many other employees and is incompatible with the development of goals that are shared by the manager and employees. Consequently, I frequently provide my definition of "expect" to employees and then use this definition repeatedly in followup discussions. This can be extremely effective in promoting employee responsibility and performance. In particular, I inform them that saying that I "expect" something from them means that the employee is fully capable of doing what is expected and that I am planning on seeing it done. This must be accompanied by sincere confidence and an understanding of shared credit and shared blame. Otherwise, the threatening use of "expect" can be implied, and the desired result cannot be obtained. However, in discussions in which an employee needs only confidence and/or assurance to succeed, this can provide strong positive incentive to accomplish what is requested. (See *Shared Credit – Shared Blame.*)

Defining "Fair"

Every manager will be exposed to the argument from an employee that something is not "fair." Everyone should realize that life is not fair. If it were, either no one would need to wear eyeglasses or we all would. Also, if life were fair, either no one would have a serious disease (such as cancer or polio) or we all would, and the bottom half of this page would not be blank. Consequently, one should not expect everything to be fair. It is also important to note that what is considered as fair by one person may not seem to be at all fair to another because of the very personal nature of our perceptions.

However, these points are not presented as a defense for failing to attempt to be fair. In truth, no matter how hard he or she tries, no manager can be completely fair. So, the best a manager can do is to diligently strive to be fair, and the manager needs to be able to understand this and to explain it to others, especially when they believe that some person or situation has not been fair. (See *The Expectation Trap.*)

In conclusion, "fair" is an ideal yet subjective term. However, it is also a necessary aspiration at all times and in all dealings to be an effective manager.

The Horse Pull

A traditional event at county fairs is one in which teams of draft horses try to pull a weighted sled between two lines within a time limit. After each round of pulls, the successful teams have weight added to the sled and try again until only one team has succeeded. While this may sound cruel, the horses display an excitement which is obvious to all observers. When they have to wait with their harnesses attached, the horses prance with their front feet as if to say that they just can't wait to be told to perform.

This effect can also be observed in people who are assigned jobs which don't challenge them and who are told to wait for a more challenging opportunity. They become restless, pace, and seek ways in which to expend their energy which don't necessarily accomplish the tasks at hand. While such assignments are sometimes unavoidable, managers must know enough to recognize the effect and to alleviate the situation as early as possible. It is just as important not to keep employees underloaded as it is not to keep them overloaded. Failure to manage this properly can be expected to result in the horse pulling with some other team.

Risks of Competition

Competition among members of work groups can be very effective as long as it is not over-emphasized and the capabilities of the competition are sufficiently equitable. However, this strategy can backfire and significantly damage morale if it is not used carefully.

For example, in a food processing plant, corn was being husked, cored, cooked, and packaged. In order to accomplish this, the corn traveled on large conveyors past a line of approximately twenty people whose job was to pick up an ear of corn and place it in one of a set of moving slots which carried the ear to a husk-removal machine. The machine could process ears without any empty slots, but a foreman observed that typically only three to five consecutive slots contained ears. The foreman pointed this out to the workers during break and wondered aloud how many consecutive slots could be filled. The workers returned to the corn line and began striving to set the consecutive ear-filled slot record. An unofficial contest developed which offset the boredom and provided a new camaraderie, and the foreman felt very proud of the idea.

For approximately a week, the workers delighted in trying to reset the record as it started at eight consecutive slots and proceeded to approximately two dozen slots. Because very few empty slots were being left by each competitor, the number of ears being husked each minute went up substantially, even to the point of overloading the next process area, which was coring. This was accommodated by sending some huskers to the coring area, and the overall plant's corn output was increased.

Then the foreman blew it by bringing in a highly-energetic and very coordinated new worker to the corn lines. Hearing of the contest, this new worker attacked the record with zeal, exceeding it the first day. Within two more days, this worker had reset the record to over fifty consecutive slots filled. The other workers surrendered, returning rapidly to their previous lower morale level and leaving many unfilled slots again. Of course the plant output declined. Realizing this, the foreman quickly negotiated another assignment for the record-busting worker and discussed this effect with the remaining workers. Fortunately, they accepted that the record-buster was atypical, and renewed their own competition, thus restoring the product flow.

The main points to consider in this example are:

1) Competition, in which each person feels they are competitive, can be constructive to productivity and morale.

2) Large rewards are not always needed. (In this case, the reward was nothing more than verbal recognition and temporary bragging rights.)

3) Overall output from a large group of people is more dependent on the *average* output than a single contributor's.

4) Complete dominance of the competition by one person can demoralize, and consequently drive out, the other competitors.

Enlightened managers will seek to obtain performance improvements through understanding of 1, 2, and 3 above but will continually monitor this risk provided by 4. In particular, the risk encountered here was not what would ordinarily have been expected. (The reader should remember that the initial result of the competition was an imbalance in shop floor loading, and the second result was identification of a need to remove a star performer from the competition.) Nevertheless, since the main purpose of management is to find improved ways to get work done, the manager should accept the risk and encourage healthy competition wherever it can be found.

A second risk of competition exists when a manager is

perceived as possessing too strong an advantage in competing with his or her peers or management, thus being considered a threat instead of a compatible resource. (Please note that "perceived" is the most important word in the preceding sentence. See *The Perception-Reality Gap*.) When perceived as a threat, the manager's effectiveness is significantly impaired, and the manager needs to find a way to establish a new perception in the view of whomever feels threatened. This is easy advice to give but is extremely difficult to accomplish. For one thing, the manager may not even be aware of the harmful perception until recovery is very difficult, if even possible. Thus, each manager needs somehow to monitor the responses of peers and organizational superiors with the specific purpose of observing reactions which might indicate others feeling threatened. When such indications are observed, the manager needs to consciously encourage the observed party and provide clear evidence of being a team player instead of a threat. The risk of this second effect is too great and should be avoided whenever possible.

Stretch Objectives vs. "Safety"

This is an important strategic point for any organization. The main issue is whether the focus is on positive incentives or negative. The employees' perception of this focus will usually determine whether the employees strive for "safety" or are willing to pursue difficult or "stretch" objectives with the risk of falling short.

When the primary behavior reinforcements are based on negative incentives, employees and managers alike learn to only subscribe to objectives which are easily met in order to avoid negative strokes. This results in the overall accomplishment level of the organization never reaching its maximum. (Those who ski at a level of never falling aren't increasing their abilities.) Yet some managers operate mainly out of fear, trying to always remain "safe". While this may actually be rewarded in the short run, it is more important than ever to be increasingly productive and progressive in the modern competitive business environment.

15

In contrast, an organization which emphasizes risk-taking and provides positive reinforcement as the main motivator encourages employees to seek ways to increase their accomplishment levels in hopes of receiving greater rewards. Knowing that risk is encouraged and that occasional failure is acceptable, most employees will consciously strive to exceed the "safe" accomplishment levels. As a consequence, the overall organizational results will automatically be improved.

Most organizations simply can't afford the luxury of failing to do their very best. Therefore, it is crucial to avoid the personal "safety" which places the overall organization at risk. In fact, some organizations actually need to provide rewards for those who have taken risk and failed (in order to encourage others to take risk). To those who have not seen outstanding or small-group performance be insufficient to sustain the success of a larger organization, this concept is hypothetical. But to those among us who have personally experienced the effect, this concept is fundamental. (Note: In sports, the best player in a game is not necessarily on the winning team.)

Hence, as a manager, one actually has an obligation to the employees and the rest of the organization to set ambitious performance objectives (as long as they are not overwhelmingly so) and to provide suitable rewards for exceeding the "safe" performance level which would otherwise have been attained. (See *"Satisfactory" Performance Is Not Good Enough.*)

Chapter II

What Values and Style Should You Exhibit?

Should you be friends with the boss? How should you react to hearsay and accomplishments of your subordinates? Should you put your job ahead of your career? What values are appropriate?

These questions are critical for managers as well as others. However, the answers are not what many pretenders to the title "manager" think. Some answers to these questions and some others are provided in the following topics. This chapter also challenges the reader to always apply practical approaches and to lead through positive example.

Be Friends With the Boss?

One tactic which is employed very effectively to further one's pay and position is to be friends with the boss even if this requires completely abandoning one's principles and values. One must, first and foremost, attend objectively to business and if you and the boss happen to also become friends, that is a bonus. But relying too heavily instead on friendship can leave one completely vulnerable when one's benefactor is transferred or otherwise leaves. (See *Too Far Too Fast.*) In fact, if you must choose between being friends with the boss and attending to business, the only real choice is attending to business. (See *Choosing Where To Take Your Hits.*) However, in nearly every workplace, examples exist which seem to illustrate that if one's only objective is to gain money and position, being friends with the boss (no matter what compromises are required) is an effective tactic. This tactic does not gain acceptance of others, though, and can impair the effectiveness of both the employee and the boss when they need to provide results through the support of others.

A most interesting and ironic example of the fallacy of artificially befriending the boss was a series of alternating male-female and female-male liaisons over a span of several years where the last symbiotic underling actually had his benefactor leave and then found himself working for the original benefactor in the series, with whom he did not have good rapport. Needless to say, he was not able to retain his artificially-gained standing and was soon on the job market.

Candor

Candor is tied hand-in-hand to integrity and is particularly necessary to be effective long-term as a manager. In fact, to gain acceptance (and retain it), a manager must provide candor to demonstrate extending trust. Some managers find that they are uncomfortable being candid, though, when asked sensitive questions. They fear that their only options are either to divulge information which should be held in confidence or to not be able to be candid at all. Instead, one of three responses can be given honestly by the manager to any sensitive question.

These three are:

1) The straight answer, if it is known and can be shared.
2) "I don't know." (If true.)
3) "I know, but I can't divulge that." (Also, if true – i.e. If asked what someone else's pay is, which the manager actually knows, the manager should *not* disclose the pay so should give this answer.)

I have personally used these three responses in several direct management and project management roles, and they have always resulted in increased credibility for me. In particular, once employees know that one of these answers will always be provided and that the manager is candid, they readily accept each response as appropriate.

Don't Act Like A Short-Timer

The definition used for "short-timer" here is a person whose employment is ending in the very near future on a known date. Hence, such a person will only continue to be a member of the organization for a short time (usually less than a month). And a true "short-timer" would be such a person whose allegiance to the employer and commitment to the assigned tasks are minimal, if they exist at all.

Behavior patterns of short-timers usually include some combination of reduced work hours, lower work quality, unwillingness to take on new assignments, and a lack of any concern for the condition of the work and the work area for whoever will inherit responsibilities which they are relinquishing. One might assume that such short-timers would only be found among employees whose jobs are being phased out, who are facing layoff, or who are part of a business which is being disbanded (or sold). On the contrary, some people who have been treated well and are voluntarily leaving a viable organization can exhibit short-timer behaviors. Why this is true may seem mysterious, but one point to understand is that the behavior does occur and seems to be much more dependent on the individual than the situation.

The most important point to understand is that short-timer behavior is observed by one's superiors, peers, and subordinates and can affect future references and one's reputation. More importantly, though, these behaviors exemplify a lack of loyalty and personal pride. They also project that the short-timer does not feel that he or she is subject to the same rules as everyone else. And what manager would want departing employees to leave with assignments uncompleted or in disarray? Instead, a conscientious person with personal pride will have an internal need to sustain his or her commitment to the employer and the job to the very end, leaving everything in the best shape possible. Doing so enables one to leave with pride and satisfaction which then carries over to whatever new position he or she fills next. It also confirms that the values which have been espoused are actually held by the conscientious person. However, the person who shows even higher commitment during the final days and hours (in order to leave everything in exceptionally good order) is not a short-timer by the above definitions, and no manager should ever behave as a short-timer!

Legal, Moral, Ethical, and Makes Business Sense

As an employee, everyone is asked to do something sometime which seems undesirable or perhaps unacceptable. Certainly one should routinely perform tasks or duties commensurate with their skills and the basic job description. However, on an exception basis, one must be prepared not to be a prima donna and to accept undesirable chores and do whatever it takes to get the job done, however mundane the task.

One model that receives great acceptance is to explain to others that it is the rightful prerogative to assign someone any task that passes the test of being legal, moral, and ethical. If the assignment passes this test, then the assignee should readily agree to do whatever he or she agrees makes business sense. If the assignment doesn't seem to make business sense, then the assignee should question the assignment (see *Loyalty*). However, if the person requesting the assignment still wants it done after being questioned, the assignee should allow for others to perhaps make mistakes and go ahead and do the task.

Several employee groups have been mentored to consider decisions through the use of this model, and each group has responded well to it. The only risk of doing so is that the employees become more concerned with the quality of decisions and can be expected to be unwilling to support decisions which don't pass the test of being legal, moral, and ethical. Consequently, managers who share this model with their employees absolutely *must* have integrity and the courage to overrule or contest decisions which fail this test. (See *It's Okay to Disagree*.)

Loyalty

Some managers mistakenly believe that loyalty means that a person will do whatever the manager tells (or asks) them to do without question or follow the manager's lead regardless of

prudence or folly. On the contrary, true loyalty requires that one try to protect the manager from mistakes. For example, instead of watching a leader walk off a cliff (and perhaps walking off behind him), a *loyal* friend or follower would attempt to stop the leader before the cliff is reached. In the workplace, a manager needs sometimes to actually stand right up and accept the boss's ire, if necessary, to prevent consequential mistakes. A good boss will value this if it is done with diplomatic firmness and correct intentions. (See *It's Okay to Disagree.*)

A significant feature of loyalty which is commonly misunderstood is its two-way nature. Loyalty must be given to be received. For two ways to demonstrate giving loyalty to employees, see *Motivation Through Compacts* and *The Manager as Publicist.*

Poise vs. Reacting Based on Hearsay

Every manager will receive a mixture of valid and completely inaccurate information. How each manager deals with information of both kinds can significantly affect his or her effectiveness. The most difficult task is to distinguish between them.

First, it must be understood that all secondhand reports of events are hearsay by definition. Consequently, if a manager receives a report of a controversial or disparaging nature (no matter how impassioned), no action should be taken without first establishing whether or not the report is correct. If the report is correct, then the manager needs to objectively determine the best corrective action to take and do so. (The most constructive action sometimes is to do nothing.) On the other hand, if the report is incorrect, the manager needs to discuss the inaccuracy of the report with the person who gave it.

Some managers fail to understand the need for poise and act immediately based on hearsay. Usually, this action follows a report from a supposedly "credible" source who the manager believes must be right every time (see *Perfection*). At other times, managers will react based on hearsay without confirming the report because it has been presented as "confidential". But too often this "confidential" information is presented as such to protect the reporter from the test of scrutiny. An equally dangerous temptation is to believe the report because it comes from several people (see *Truth – It Cannot Be Established By Vote*).

The most glaring example I can give of the fallacy of hearsay happened to me when I was the hiring manager for the first time for a promotional position. The position was described and applications were requested in an open memo to all groups in the business unit, and approximately a dozen applications were received. However, my boss soon took me aside and shared with me that one of the candidates had told him "in confidence" that the successful candidate had already been picked prior to the interviews and that this was unfair. As a newcomer to the business unit, I knew very little about most of the applicants, so I asked him to write the name down and keep it in his top desk drawer until after I hired someone for the position. We agreed to discuss the name then. So, after I had agreement on terms with the successful candidate, I asked him to share the name with me, but he declined. As it turned out, he had had two more such entreaties resulting in a list of three alleged unfairly-selected winners, but none of the three actually had gotten the job! To this day, their identities are not known to me, but I still appreciate having had a manager with sufficient poise not to overreact to unfounded hearsay. Every manager should develop such poise.

Putting Your Job Ahead of Your Career (and Vice-Versa)

This concept seems to be simple and self-explanatory, but it is a result of one's fundamental value set and work ethic. Some people are so dedicated that, regardless of the value or futility of providing loyalty to an organization, they will often strive for total perfection on their immediate tasks. Even knowing that such extraordinary commitment at least temporarily interferes with their ability to cultivate their career growth, these conscientious workers are often unable to cut back. This ethic is actually valuable in any organization and needs to be carefully monitored and directed by the respective manager to assure equity between present job assignments and the individual's career. Regrettably, many managers undervalue this attribute and, for their own personal gain, milk these employees for all they can.

In the reverse effect, many employees pay strict attention to determining what activities are expected to most effectively accelerate their career growth (at least pay and position). In their pursuit of such accelerated career gains, these employees don't actually care what is best for the rest of the organization and can provide serious business performance handicaps. These same employees also become highly vulnerable when organizational changes occur or their sponsor leaves. (See *Too Far Too Fast*.)

The best approach one should pursue is to somehow maintain a delicate balance between job and career. This is not easy, though, and requires serious periodic attention.

Seek Unity

An error committed frequently by managers is to overpower or overrule honest dissent or disagreement. Such an error is obvious when it occurs, and it divides groups into supportive and non-supportive members. However, more subtle effects often occur in meetings or project management which divide a team and need careful attention by the manager. In particular, the "dotted-line" organizational connections on temporary or project-based assignments may enable those from whom support is needed to give less than their all without any significant consequences to them. This is mainly due to the lack of direct authority of the project or matrix manager over these team members. Thus, the responsible manager is compelled to rely heavily on information, persuasion, and team spirit to inspire everyone to give their very best to the job at hand. In order to accomplish this, the project leader needs to use his or her full creativity to develop and nurture a feeling of unity in every member of the team. Team-building and project management are both significant disciplines, but neither can be done with any success without first seeking and developing unity in the team.

Merely stating a desire to have unity is not sufficient. The leader or manager must carefully watch for signs of the lack of unity, especially during team activities. One sign is a clear lack of concentration or attentive behavior during team meetings by some or all of the team members. The effect of being "all fired up" is widely understood and is expected to be followed by good results. However, being "all fired down" is often ignored or unrecognized. When part or all of a team is unenthusiastic, the team leader needs to determine constructive strategies to restore unity and enthusiasm as quickly as possible.

To summarize, the need for unity is much more widespread than only temporary or project assignments, and obtaining it may be very difficult in some instances. Regardless of the difficulty of obtaining full agreement or total support on assignments (and even if it can't be completely realized), seeking unity at all times is necessary for success in management.

Shared Credit – Shared Blame

Since the primary measure of a manager's effectiveness is the accomplishments of his or her subordinates, the manager should be delighted to have the employee do well and share the credit. (See *The Manager as Publicist*.) However, if a manager is to err in sharing credit, it should be by placing extra credit on the employee and not by failing to share it. (See *Credit Stealing*.) Also, sharing credit is crucial in promoting teamwork. Through sharing of credit, a team will work more effectively to accomplish the common goals and will tend to want every member of the team to succeed so that the team is in turn successful. Thus, sharing credit will tend to motivate a team to be self-managed. This is a powerful effect and is used effectively by many prominent leaders.

On the other hand, many managers are completely unwilling to accept a share of the blame if an employee does *not* do well. Yet

25

it is the job of the manager to provide proper work assignments, coaching, and assistance as necessary to give the employee the best possible opportunity to do well. If an employee does not do well despite actually trying to while the manager has not done these three things, the manager actually owns the greater share of the blame. However, without engaging in finger-pointing to quantify this effect, it suffices to say that the manager and the employee each own a share of the blame. This should serve as incentive for each manager to strive for success of *all* employees.

One might note that successful leaders tend to delegate credit for success (knowing that they still share in it) and take blame themselves for their team's failures (knowing that this develops loyalty). All managers need to be leaders.

Stay on the Learning Curve

In earlier years, the essentials of a particular job assignment or department could be mastered and would hold a person in good stead long-term. However, in this age of the computer, rapid changes occur in the available tools for the job, manufacturing techniques, and analysis techniques to measure results of your own organization as well as the competition. Also, the legal requirements with which managers must comply continue to change. Still, the successful manager must continue to set an example of forward thinking and vision and must inspire others to keep pace with the changing environment. Consequently, every manager now needs to continually increase his or her skills.

A conventional comparison model for discussing employee mastery of job tasks is the learning curve by which the productivity on an assigned task initially increases rapidly and then more slowly approaches a maximum level. With improvement of understanding or techniques, it is possible to reset the curve and thus elevate the maximum level. This makes it possible to maintain a rapid increase for a longer period and to attain higher ultimate results. Since obtaining results through others is the main job of a manager (See *The Manager as Publicist*), for all managers to stay on the learning curve and to keep their employees on this curve with them is an obvious necessity to remain successful in today's competitive environment. Ironically, there is no established checklist regarding what one will need to learn in the future. Instead, part of the needed learning will be which topics need to be learned next.

Strategic Information Leaks

A manager received an employee on probation through a departmental reorganization. This employee had a long-standing history of inadequate performance in one category. The manager responsibly reviewed the probation terms with the employee immediately and confirmed that the employee was informed that failure to meet the terms could be expected to result in termination. Still the employee failed to comply and provide satisfactory performance. Because the policies of the company in this set of events required extensive documentation, review, and signatures to terminate the employee, termination of the employee took more than two months after the manager's initial recommendation.

During this period between recommendation and termination of the employee, the manager was confronted by a peer of the employee who said, "You are costing me money." When asked by the manager for an explanation, the peer continued, "I bet $10 that you would fire that employee within three months." The peer further stated that the general employee base knew of the probation, its cause, and the employee's failure to improve. They also considered the manager to be fair but strong enough to stand behind requirements. Thus, they were watching to see if their perception of the manager was correct or if even this manager would fail to effectively resolve the issue of the employee's performance gap.

The manager was trapped between confidentiality of the employee's job status and losing his own personal credibility. In order to try to preserve both, the manager decided to "leak" information. So, without disclosing the employee's status, the manager asked the peer whether the bet required actually sending the person home within three months of the employee's arrival in his group, or recommending this action within three months. The peer responded that the recommendation would result in winning the bet. Though this action had already been taken, the manager said that he couldn't officially disclose any information. But from the manager's question, the peer discreetly concluded that the employee's performance was somehow being addressed, and the manager's credibility was maintained.

In another example, a clever interviewer once called a manager to discuss a former employee who had not been a good performer, and the former employee gave permission to answer the interviewer's questions. The interviewer, after confirming the employee's previous job title and employment dates, extracted from the manager that an opening existed in the manager's group as they spoke. She then asked if the manager wanted to rehire the former employee. The manager responded "Well, ... " and was cut off by a quick "Never mind." The interviewer knew that the manager had, through only slight hesitation, leaked that the employee was not a strong performer.

Another way that information can strategically be "leaked" is when a manager who normally gives open denials to rumors, responds with "no comment." This response must be used very carefully, though, or it can be interpreted as confirmation of the

rumor *and* okay for public discussion.

The point of these paragraphs is that there are times when a manager needs not to reveal complete information, yet still needs to allow others to not be totally uninformed. When, in the manager's judgment, this situation occurs, a strategic "leak" can be effective. It is important to understand, though, that this should be used carefully and infrequently. In particular, the "leak" must be provided only to discriminating and trustworthy inquirers who have some reason to know the information. Otherwise, no confidentiality at all can be maintained. (For a related concept, see *Candor*.)

Values – Stated vs. Projected vs. Actual

It has already been stated that total integrity is absolutely mandatory to be an effective manager and that all managers need to be leaders. It should also be understood that a critical facet of leadership is the ability to inspire others to achieve that which they would not achieve by themselves. In order to be able to so inspire others long-term, the leader must be trusted by those being led. Integrity alone will not assure this. In addition, the leader

29

must possess indisputable sincerity.

Merely stating that one possesses particular values will not suffice. Nor will such statements accompanied by the most carefully practiced gestures and facial expressions. Just as a horse can sense which people fear it, those being led can quickly ascertain any differences between stated values, projected values, and one's actual values. Attempts to misrepresent one's values are an insult to those who see through the charade and can create a significant gap between the attempter and his or her audience.

In summary, a manager needs to be sincere in all his or her dealings in order to be effective. (See *Candor* and *Integrity*.) Also, the manager's actual values must match with those stated and projected.

Chapter III

Ten Common Misconceptions

We may all realize that common sense isn't really common. But other misconceptions are not recognized by many managers. And these can seriously diminish the manager's effectiveness. A few of these are addressed here, and each manager can probably identify other misconceptions to offset.

Focusing on What It Looks Like Someone Is Doing Instead of What Is Getting Done

Some employees are particularly productive through organization without ever seeming to hustle. Others have mastered the art of constructive laziness and will always seek the simplest and most straightforward among a set of possible solutions. Yet some managers will downgrade such employees or openly encourage them to "look busy." These same managers will often praise those who look busy at all times regardless of their actual accomplishment. Confusing motion with action this way may be good enough for an exercise class, but the measure of success in business is results. (You cannot sell two products each half-completed, but you likely can sell one product fully completed.)

While this discussion may seem hypothetical, the organized employee can often quietly provide astounding results without being duly rewarded. Also, many managers wish to strictly enforce a "no visiting" philosophy in the mistaken belief that conversations between employees during work time automatically reduce productivity. This is directly contradictory to the effect of peer discussions as discussed later in this chapter. (See *Peers – Definition and Frequency of Intellectual Exchange*.)

One example of this topic is contained in the question of whether someone is paid for what they do or for what they know. In one situation, a well-paid engineer seemed to be extremely casual at his job and was observed frequently reading with his feet propped up. A widely-held perception was that this engineer did not work hard, was probably not worth his pay, and must have been protected by someone higher in the organization for political reasons. However, one of the resident skeptics once needed expert information regarding vacuum technology and was referred to the engineer in question. The engineer listened to the skeptic's description of the problem and accompanying questions and then replied that he had read an applicable article within the previous week. He then pulled out three references and began comparing the most recent articles on the subject. Within twenty minutes, he told the skeptic what changes to make. His

recommendations were exactly right and saved the skeptic approximately three months of data collection and analysis. Subsequently the skeptic pointedly watched for similar results from the engineer and found that he read approximately four-fifths of the time but saved multiples of his wage by making other people more efficient. This is a case where it was to his employer's advantage to pay him for what he knew.

Another example of the fallacy of focusing on what it looks like someone is doing occurred in a cannery where a foreman was responsible for the production output from two different but adjacent product lines. In this instance, the foreman realized that the product flow was sporadic for both products and this caused frequent reassignment of the workers. Also, a lack of ownership in the results by the workers coupled with minimal training was resulting in allowance of product containers which were improperly spaced for a wrapping machine. The improper spacing had caused frequent mechanical jamming of the machine for years, so each foreman had received extensive training on repair of the machine. By training the three closest workers to watch the product spacing and remove extra containers (which could be reinserted later), the foreman essentially eliminated machine downtime on his shift. Then he had another worker time the product flow to calibrate product stoppage and restart for minimal lost time. These two factors enabled the foreman to run both product lines alternately with only one crew, increased employee morale (they didn't have to be reassigned every shift), and gave more product output on that shift than on both other shifts combined. However, in one discussion with a manager who only saw the foreman at random times, the manager lauded the foreman of the next shift for his ability to repair the machine and downgraded the higher-producing foreman for spending time talking to the employees. Even when told that his own records would show the higher output, the manager was unable to understand that his focus was wrong.

The primary lesson to be learned here is that good managers use business-related measures for employee evaluation – not appearances and activity levels.

Leadership vs. Followership

As a young man, I was repeatedly told by graduates of a prominent military academy that mastering followership was necessary to later development of leadership. My position is that this couldn't be further from the truth. In fact, some of history's greatest leaders were renowned for not being good followers. And the main difference between leaders and followers is fundamental to their basic personalities.

It is true that both leadership and followership behavior can be taught, but when the chips are down, each individual will respond according to his or her inherent characteristics. In other words, while a follower can be aware of the principles, tactics, and behaviors of leadership, when the need arises unexpectedly, this person will still be a follower. On the other hand, even if reluctant, a person with inherent leadership characteristics will lead when needed, particularly on a temporary basis to assure success of some project or effort which is important to him or her. But significant difficulty can be expected when a follower is designated as a manager and tries to mold his or her employees to also be followers. Instead, managers need to be leaders who inspire others to lead.

One of the signals which identifies a follower-manager is contained in the language chosen to designate his or her fill-in when expecting to be gone (on vacation, on a business trip, etc.). Leaders consider themselves responsible or accountable and hence designate their fill-ins as "responsible" for duties. In contrast, followers designate their fill-ins as "in charge" (because that's how they view themselves).

In conclusion, management needs leaders, and the oft-repeated practice of promoting followers to management positions with the belief that they can be converted to leaders is a serious mistake. Instead, managers need to recognize that the difference between leaders and followers is fundamental and endeavor to assign both correctly.

Which way did they go?

How fast were they going?

How many of them were there?

I must find them ...I'm their leader!

Note: The origin of this quotation is unknown; it was displayed on bulletin boards at a previous employer.

Line Management vs. Matrix Management

Surprisingly, some veteran managers have no understanding of matrix management. When confronted with the need to get results from people who aren't under them in the formal organizational structure, they immediately want to reorganize so that they will have control. This has an element of sadness to it because these managers never experience the emotional lift provided by the success of an interdepartmental team effort.

In essence, in line management, a manager can personally define goals and objectives and rely on position power to assure that employee efforts are directed to meet these goals and objectives because of the clear definition of authority over his or her subordinates. Military discipline clearly requires line management with strict obedience to orders when under fire in the field, and many managers who were in the military are highly conditioned to this approach.

In comparison, matrix management is a formal organizational approach in which the organizational chart does not apply directly (with agreement and approval of affected line managers) so that the matrix manager has commensurate authority and responsibilities for employee support and administrative functions (such as performance evaluations and pay changes). Nevertheless, because of the temporary nature of matrix assignments, the main tool for matrix management is persuasion based on reason, logic, and personal acceptance of the requesting manager. Teamwork, cooperation, and group determination of the goals and objectives not only are results of matrix management, but are absolutely necessary for its success.

While the above paragraphs may seem to imply that all managers can be slotted as either line managers or matrix managers, many managers possess the versatility to excel at both. In fact, managers who follow the concepts presented in this book will seldom rely on position power and hence will be able to learn, and be comfortable with, matrix management. They also will be effective as line managers.

Management vs. the "Technical Guru"

This is a subject which has been discussed often during hiring negotiations. The subject arises because many managers don't fully appreciate the difference between the skills needed to be an individual performer and those needed to inspire stronger performance from others. Because of this, many managers chartered with hiring a subordinate manager seek the best accountant to manage accountants, the best salesman to manage salesmen, the best scientist to manage scientists, etc. My contention is that these "technical gurus" are considerably more valuable to the organization when performing in their field of expertise and should be properly rewarded for that instead of being miscast as managers. The skills needed to excel as a manager are not the same as those to excel as an accountant, a salesman, or a scientist. And placing management responsibility on the "technical guru" is detrimental to that individual and the organization as a whole. The individual misses the satisfaction of the successes which established him or her as the expert, and the organization misses the leadership it needs. Yet this concept is still widely misunderstood.

Often, the "technical guru" is sought because the hiring manager believes that choice to be "safe" because the guru will know how to train or provide technical leadership to the subordinates. This risk-avoidance leads to meddling instead of delegation and an inability to develop subordinates to become competent managers (because their role models and would-be mentors are technical experts instead).

In closing, the strongest "technical guru" possesses those skills because of a combination of talent, experience, training, and desire and should be assigned where that combination is the most valuable. In comparison, the best candidate for the management role is a leader with the ability to understand the tasks at hand, determine the capabilities of the employees, and match those the best to provide optimum business performance.

Mentoring

This is normally considered a unilateral management activity by which one provides guidance and information to subordinates. But this is not merely appropriate behavior for management. Instead, we each have areas in which we turn to others for information regardless of their positions in the formal structure. In doing so, we are seeking mentoring from those others, if only in their main areas of expertise. We also have our own knowledge areas in which others turn to us. In essence, this constitutes an effect by which we each provide mentoring to one another without necessarily realizing that we are doing so.

What is proposed here is that, in the workplace, each employee or manager is part of a team that should work as a cohesive unit to be the best possible. Therefore, the obligation to provide mentoring is not limited to downward in the formal structure but extends upward, downward, and laterally. Certainly loyalty, as defined earlier, dictates that subordinates also will want to have their management be as informed as possible and will thus want to share information and knowledge openly with their management (referred to as upward mentoring).

For a note of irony on this subject, see *Punctuality vs. Efficient Use of Time.*

Peers – Definition and Frequency of Intellectual Exchange

I encountered this concept while researching the paper on management of scientists and engineers. Most managers operate under the assumption that each employee's peers can be found at the same level as the employee can on an official organization chart and that their parallel positions according to the formal structure establish them as peers. What those managers don't realize is that *only the employee* can determine who his or her peers are and that those peers can be from any part of the formal structure.

Coupled with this information is the well-documented, but little-known concept that the creativity and productivity of engineers and scientists increase with approximately three to five conversations per week with their peers on intellectual topics of their choosing, whether directly pertinent to their individual assignments or not. In fact, creativity is definitely enhanced when a peer group free-wheels on blue-sky discussions regarding one member's efforts and tries to extend their ideas to a complete logical extreme. And productivity of each participant is normally increased because of their excitement from the discourse. Of course the pertinence of this effect is not limited to engineers and scientists. I have also seen groups of assemblers increase their job performance and satisfaction through similar exchanges in which they shared ideas regarding techniques and processes. Yet many managers instead consider such discourses at best wasted time and at worst a performance issue.

What needs to be understood is that people's creativity and productively are actually enhanced by a proper frequency of intellectual exchanges by employees and those who *they* define as their peers.

Power vs. Authority
(vs. Perception vs. Responsibility)

Many managers believe that power and authority are basically synonymous. This couldn't be farther from the truth, and one way in which the distinction is clear is in the comparison of the formal and informal structures in organizations. People high in the formal structure have defined authority and may or may not have power. In contrast, people accepted as elevated in the informal structure may have no defined authority but can possess significant power as evidenced by the effect they can have through influence and persuasion.

The key to this comparison lies in understanding that authority is needed in a formal structure to accompany responsibility but that power is actually a result of perception. In other words, if

39

you perceive that someone possesses sufficient power to control your actions, they do. This power is granted to that someone by you. But authority is granted by someone else with even higher authority (it usually can be traced to legal authority or power of the purse).

The value of this is that while each assignment as a manager carries a degree of authority with it, the manager needs also to learn to obtain allegiance and acceptance from subordinates and peers. This will provide the manager with a power that is often much more valuable than position authority.

Punctuality vs. Efficient Use of Time

In one work environment, a newly-formed team was assigned a very complex project. In order to develop cohesiveness and common objectives, the team agreed to develop a code of conduct. During the ensuing discussions, considerable time was spent trying to reach agreement on how to *require* punctuality of all members at all team meetings. Some members contended that, while punctuality is courteous and desirable, the total time from the planned beginning time of a meeting to its actual completion accurately reflects the actual cost of the meeting. The strongest advocates of punctuality were completely nonchalant regarding the time the meeting would end. After approximately three hours of debate, the team hammered out an agreement to include the rule "Be on time – Start on time." Ironically, the next guideline proposed was "Everyone should serve as a mentor for one another" which is much more important for an organization's sustained success. However, the meaning of "mentor" was not known to the strongest advocates of punctuality, so this topic was shelved within three minutes (too quickly for a dictionary to be retrieved at a dead run).

The scenario described above constituted a significant contradiction and resulted in a confrontation between team members which caused some to re-examine their basic value sets. In particular, the non-advocates of punctuality developed a stronger commitment to it. However, the punctuality advocates

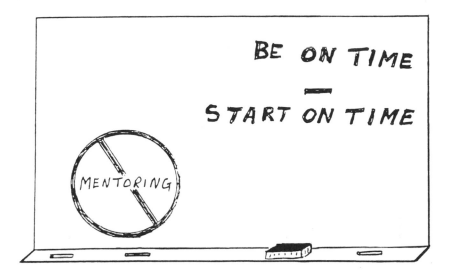

did not respond similarly to their compatriots' concern for efficient use of time, and most of the meetings, though starting on time, were not completed with efficiency or on schedule.

In conclusion, punctuality is a matter of courtesy which should be honored. However, a short, efficient meeting which starts five or less minutes late is more cost-effective than a meeting which starts on time and ends significantly later. So if a manager must choose, efficient use of meeting time is better business than punctuality. Thus, each manager should definitely monitor the clock and strive for both, but informed managers will not value punctuality more than efficient use of time.

Speed vs. Quality

Most managers and employees face deadlines of one sort or another, and in some instances, missing the deadline means lost revenue. (Would you subscribe to a newspaper that regularly published Sunday's paper on Monday?) In manufacturing, quality vs. quantity is always a question to consider. However, the real answer to the question is to find a way to provide a quality product in the scheduled quantity at the scheduled time. In other

41

words, the real key to success is balance, as has been emphasized elsewhere in this manuscript.

In some efforts, managers lose sight of the balance described above because of the lack of a well-defined schedule or a lack of concern for schedule conflicts. As an example, annual budgets and other planning documents are frequently requested against tight deadlines with the ground rules unknown to the assignees until the assignment is made. Yet the basic time lines and formats are usually definable months in advance. The managers who procrastinate on defining these then typically require a result based on speed. By not providing the ground rules earlier, they sacrifice quality on efforts which could have provided an opportunity to give serious consideration to optimization of the overall business. Keep in mind, though, that allowing such time and accepting higher quality planning for subordinates requires managers to relinquish some control and delegate. (See *Delegation* and *Decisions at the Lowest Appropriate Level.*)

The point to understand is that the need to balance speed and quality exists in nearly every job, not just a few, and maintaining this balance is a significant challenge. However, each manager needs to pursue this balance continually. The primary misconception often exhibited is that this balance applies only to a select few assignments and is not important in most other assignments.

Twenty Years' Experience
vs.
One Year's Experience Twenty Times

This concept is almost self-explanatory, but quickly describes a major pitfall. In particular, many managers seek candidates for hire with numerous years of experience. However, in an age of rapid change, what was learned several years ago often is inappropriate today. Also, the candidate with one year's experience repeated several times (through not changing) will lack the versatility and creativity which may actually be needed.

Consequently, a candidate with fewer years of experience, but in several different relevant assignments, can often easily provide stronger performance.

At one job, a manager had been such for twenty years but had spent the last several of these in one stagnant assignment. His information was not at all current on several fundamental topics about which new information was available, and this reduced his effectiveness considerably. He was a good man, though, and when given a new assignment was willing to learn from subordinates who had less, but more relevant, experience.

The point of issue is that the relevance and applicability of experience is much more important than the number of years.

"When in Rome ..."

We trained hard — but every time we were beginning to form up into teams, we would be reorganized. ... I was to learn later in life that we tend to meet any new situation by reorganizing, and a wonderful method it can be for creating the illusion of progress while producing confusion, inefficiency, and demoralization.

Petronius Arbiter 210 B.C.

Note: This quotation is unsubstantiated and was displayed on bulletin boards at a previous employer. It has been included because of its relevance to the workplace.

Tips for Strategic Managers

Chapter IV

Of Decision-Making and Differences of Opinion

While decision-making is a widely covered topic, still too few managers actually have the knack. Part of this is because of a mistaken belief that popular decisions will automatically be good ones or that the manager must exhibit his control or superiority by making all of the important decisions. One needs to remember that no one can make all good or correct decisions. Instead, it is widely accepted that the difference between good managers and others primarily lies only in the percentage of decisions which turn out to be good ones (Note: Good decisions are not necessarily those without risk.)

Also, disagreement is encouraged or presented as healthy in most organizations, according to philosophy statements, while actually not being accepted at all in some of these same organizations. Managers need to realize that penalizing for honest disagreement stifles open communication and can limit business results.

Conflicting Goals

What do you do when called upon to meet goals which conflict? Perhaps this seems to be hypothetical, but this effect occurs frequently in most managers' experiences.

An example is when a manager is called upon to meet an aggressive deadline necessitating added expense while also being called upon to minimize expenses. In such a case, the manager should determine which of the conflicting goals is the most important and then decide accordingly, letting reason prevail and accepting whatever results from not meeting the less important goal. (See *When Reason and Rules Conflict* and *Choosing Where to Take Your Hits*.) While this may seem straightforward, some managers are stymied by conflicting goals. This is unfortunate, because this situation gives the manager an opportunity to demonstrate the ability to lead and to make decisions. (See *Stretch Objectives vs. "Safety."*)

Decisions by Committee

This seems ideal in a democracy. However, such a decision process discourages taking risk. It also robs many prospective good managers of the opportunity to make individual mistakes from which they can learn much more effectively than by trying to assume a limited share of the responsibility of a committee's suboptimal decision. In a facilitating role, decisions by committee can be effective. But in many situations, they can be disastrous. Each manager must develop sufficient judgment to determine when this approach is inappropriate and then exercise the courage to prevent it.

Decisions at the Lowest Appropriate Level

This is a particularly effective approach, especially when the decision parameters are non-general and are best known by personnel other than the manager who might be called upon or otherwise believe himself (or herself) to be responsible for the decision in question. However, those with the most pertinent knowledge have the highest probability of making the best decision, and employees who find decisions delegated to them characteristically develop personal ownership of the results. This ownership often assures good business results even when the decision might not seem to be the absolute best one.

Not only is it prudent to have all decisions made at the lowest appropriate level in the organization, but each manager has an obligation to develop good decision-making ability in his employees, both for their personal growth and in case decisions must be made in the manager's absence for sickness, vacation, etc.

A Helpful Decision-making Criterion

Employees and managers at all levels should be conditioned to consider the following whenever a significant decision is to be made. Specifically, they should think in terms of what decision they would make if they either owned the company themselves or, more strongly, were starting a new competing company to take the business away from the present company. An employee named Smith should be asked, "How would this decision be made at SmithCo across the street if they wanted to take our business away?" This question frequently leads to a different decision than originally expected and always increases the employee's sensation of personal ownership in both the decision and the overall success of the company.

Depending on preference, the employee's first or last name can be used. For expample, from Mr. Don Sudo Name, the fictional company could be called "DonCo" or "NameCo." Most employees will later refer to what they would do at "NameCo" whenever they face difficult decisions.

Allowing Others to Make Mistakes

Every employee rather automatically considers it only fair to be allowed to make mistakes. However, it is not automatic to grant the same tolerance for mistakes by others, particularly those above them on the organizational chart. One must learn to tolerate mistakes from everyone in the workplace including subordinates, peers, and superiors. This is not to say that mistakes in the workplace should be encouraged or that it is acceptable for anyone to consistently make mistakes, but none of us can perform flawlessly. (See *Perfection*.) Consequently we must allow each other to make a reasonable number of mistakes. However, this basic concept does not excuse (or encourage acceptance of) dishonesty.

Choosing Where to Spend Your Bullets

Every manager will have times when he or she has a strong want or need to obtain support from someone else in which a compromise is in order. Since compromise is difficult and possibly not even viable in some situations, the manager will find that occasionally old debts, markers, favors, or whatever other articles of persuasion are available need to be expended to obtain the needed result. No one has a limitless supply of such articles, so the manager must budget his or her use of them. This is commonly described as choosing where to spend your bullets.

Note: This concept is similar to the next topic, *Choosing Where to Take Your Hits*, but slightly different because this effect can reduce your future bargaining power but brings no immediate consequences.

Choosing Where to Take Your Hits

Every employee encounters situations where meeting all requests or demands on the job is impossible. In these situations, negotiations can often remove part of the list, enabling the employee to satisfactorily comply with the remaining tasks. However, in some instances, one is not able to negotiate sufficient relief to accommodate the full remaining list of tasks. In such circumstances, the only option available is to choose which items to leave uncompleted and accept the consequences. This is usually referred to as "choosing where to take your hits."

In other situations, managers often find that they must choose between doing what's right for some but not all of their employees, their management, their company, and perhaps even society in general. For example, when called upon to do something for their management which is illegal or in opposition to corporate policy, managers must choose whether to suffer the boss's wrath or to possibly be held accountable by the law or corporate management. (This choice is easy if one understands the information provided under *Legal, Moral, Ethical, and Makes Business Sense.*)

Other circumstances can generate the same dilemma with lesser consequences. For example, a manager may need a decision to resolve some urgent issue but be unable to reach anyone who normally has the authority to make the decision. In this situation, the manager must choose either to make the decision or to leave an urgent issue unresolved. The better choice usually is to make the decision and inform the person with authority later, but this needs to be determined on a case-by-case basis. Regardless of the alternative chosen, the manager in this situation can expect to have to answer either for assuming the authority to decide or for failing to resolve the issue. Hence, the manager must choose which "hit" to take. (Notice, failure to make a decision to resolve the issue actually constitutes having made a decision not to decide.)

Hopefully, the above explanations are clear and helpful. *Every* manager will be faced with the basic dilemma in some form, and the choices made can be important.

It's Okay to Disagree

Disagreement not only can be healthy, but often provides avoidance of mistakes or better understanding of the decisions with which one disagrees. An employee or coworker who sees a potential wrong decision actually has an obligation to discuss the decision, and the owner of the decision should honor this obligation and provide a defensible case or reconsider (See *Allowing Others to Make Mistakes*). If the disagreement is erroneous but sincere, the owner of the decision needs to allow the person questioning the decision to be mistaken and to present a suitable explanation why the decision is valid. This does not mean that all decisions should be challenged, and the disagreement needs to be presented in an objective, businesslike manner. Confrontational responses by the decision owner or the questioner of that decision will often only lead to bad relations. A very effective position to find yourself in is to be considered someone who will stand behind defensible decisions but who also is *susceptible to reason* when disagreement exists and a decision is not strongly defensible.

One-Parameter Decision-Making

This is a very dangerous practice which is all too common in the workplace. Some decisions are straightforward and should actually be made with minimum analysis. However, some decisions are complex or can easily be made wrongly without viewing the possible ramifications or considering several factors. Despite this, *many decisions are made on the basis of only one parameter though they clearly should not be.* (Would anyone buy leaded gasoline for a car needing unleaded based only on the single parameter known as the purchase price?)

As an example of common mistakes regarding this concept, indirect labor staffing levels are often stipulated in accordance with historical proportionality to direct labor staffing levels. However, significant changes in the workplace due to automation can reduce the number of direct labor employees (or touch labor) needed to provide a fixed product output level. Yet the very people (indirect staff) who are responsible for the reduced direct labor, through implementing automation or other process improvements, later find their own employment in jeopardy because of their management's reliance on the historical ratios. The logical extreme of this would be for the indirect staff to make such fantastic improvements that the production process was totally automated and infinite output could then be achieved with no employees. In the real world, this management strategy either causes the indirect employees to have severe insecurity about their jobs or to apply caution limiting improvements so that their jobs are not as easily jeopardized. Neither outcome is desirable, so it behooves managers to not apply ratios without understanding the logic, both past and present, behind them. (See *When Reason and Rules Conflict.*) Instead, multiple parameters should always be sought and evaluated as a normal part of the process for significant decisions.

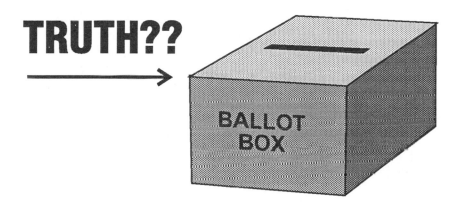

Truth – It Cannot Be Established By Vote

This concept came to my attention originally over the assertion that a manager had made a particular statement to a job candidate (during an interview) to which the candidate took issue. The manager was confronted by his boss with the allegation that five other people had told the boss that they heard the statement. As it turned out, the interviews for the position had been private interviews held in a closed room and could not have been heard by the five others. Also, the accused manager had not even participated in any of the interviews. Yet his boss still considered the hearsay from five people as more convincing than the lone word of the accused manager.

While this is a most glaring example of the obvious error of trying to determine truth by vote, the effect seems to occur sometime in nearly every workplace. And it seems to happen so easily that every manager needs not only to be cognizant of the effect, but to carefully guard against it by carefully considering if the majority could actually *know* the truth. Often, they cannot.

What's The Best Thing To Do Now?

A novice manufacturing engineer worked for an excellent senior engineer who taught this concept by example. The senior engineer's response to bad news at times was almost classic and followed the subsequent pattern several times. The effect would begin with the senior engineer sitting at his desk with his back to the entrance to his office. The novice would approach him from one side and deliver bad news. The senior engineer would then stand suddenly, propelling his chair backward, clench his fists tightly, and emit a strong terse expression. His face would be red and his knuckles white, as if he squeezed the blood from his hands up to his face. He would stand very still, then slowly relax his hands, and the blood would seem to drain from his face back to his hands. Exhibiting composure, the senior engineer would then say, "All right. That's already happened. What's the best thing to do now?" With the full attention of the novice, he would then provide mentoring to develop a recovery solution or a contingency plan.

As a manager, the use of this question can help one maintain poise and objectivity at the most crucial times. It also can help to stimulate creativity of the people with the most intimate view of the problem at hand, even for routine decisions. The senior engineer discussed above has provided this as a legacy without necessarily knowing that he has done so.

When Reason and Rules Conflict

All rules were originated for some reason. However, a strong allegiance exists for rule-based logic, meaning that many people consider rules as sacred. While rules serve a definite purpose, it is impossible to develop rules which cover all situations or changes. Consequently, we must all consider reason itself to be of greater value than the rules. This does not mean that rules should be discarded but that questioning, reviewing, and changing rules is a normal sequence of events and, in fact, the only way that the rules can actually serve their real purpose, both in business and society. (Note: *Rules* required racial segregation and exclusion of women from most leadership roles in America earlier in this century: *Reason* resulted in the present integrated society and equal opportunity regardless of gender. Without this prevailing of reason over rules, many outstanding performers in today's workplace would never have been allowed the chance to so perform.)

Tips for Strategic Managers

Chapter V

Twenty Effects Which Are Not Commonly Understood

H umorous cartoons and homilies can be found in most workplaces and usually only serve to provide a quick laugh. Some of these actually can provide some fun and camaraderie at work. Several concepts presented in this chapter are based on humor but are still pertinent. The others are not necessarily humorous, but can help one considerably to become a strategic manager. In fact, the material presented in this chapter has widespread applicability and includes the most-requested entries in this book.

The main trick is to splice these concepts into one's daily routine with an appropriate blend of humor and seriousness.

The Alligator-Mouth Syndrome

Everyone finds themselves voluntarily oversubscribed at times. For example, it is easy to underestimate the difficulty of an assignment and to agree to unmeetable schedules or accomplishments.

This I refer to as allowing one's alligator mouth to overload his or her hummingbird back end, and discussion of this effect can bring considerable humor to the workplace while also reminding everyone how easy it actually is to overcommit yourself.

The "Confusing Information with Knowledge" Trap

Many managers consider themselves to be well informed on subjects on which they are not. The fact that they are not is completely understandable because the available knowledge in most fields of endeavor changes very rapidly in this technological age, and the manager has only limited time to try to keep up because of the demands of his or her administrative chores. Consequently, a trap exists in which the manager can easily confuse a smattering of information (which is liable to be incomplete and outdated) with actual knowledge. It is much too easy for the manager to believe that this limited information actually equates to sufficiently comprehensive knowledge to enable the manager to make sound decisions. Consequently, the manager who has fallen into the trap typically makes decisions which should actually be delegated to someone else. (See *Decisions at the Lowest Appropriate Level.*) Knowing that this trap exists, the manager should try not to fall into it.

The Curse of Duty

This concept is difficult to put into words concisely. However, it basically comprises a set of obligations one has if blessed with a sufficiently strong combination of intelligence, knowledge, and opportunity. Anyone possessing such a combination needs to apply their intelligence and knowledge to assure that the society in general is benefitted by leaders with proper values. While this may seem almost an aristocratic philosophy, it is not. Instead, those fortunate enough to have the advantage of the capability and the chance to learn are obligated to apply the information which has been provided them because of commitment from earlier generations. They also are obligated to provide continuation of the knowledge legacy to the next generation. Essentially, this basic duty is firmly rooted in the early survival of humanity through family and tribal behaviors and constitutes a modified application of extended-family values.

Because intelligence and education do not necessarily correlate with assertiveness or a desire to lead, the obligation described above becomes a duty in the old-fashioned sense. Even for those who do seek leadership, events can sometimes make one wonder if the rewards are worth the trouble because of the actions of others. During these times especially, the curse of duty applies so that integrity and truth can prevail.

Another aspect of the curse of duty is that if the right people fail to step up to the responsibilities described, positions of authority will eagerly be filled by the wrong people – with damage to the general society a guaranteeable result.

> **"Doing a good job around here is like wetting your pants in a dark wool suit — you get a warm feeling all over, but nobody notices."**

Note: This saying was posted on bulletin boards at a previous workplace, but is applicable in far too many work environments. The originator is unknown.

Environmental Dependence

This is an effect which is disclaimed or subdued by many people but which is completely obvious in some others. Essentially, it is a fundamental effect by which people's morale and accomplishments are tied to their environment, particularly including the sociological environment. The ingredients of this sociological environment which most strongly influence morale and accomplishment levels are incentives and reinforcements which are provided. Every manager must be able to appropriately use both positive and negative incentives, but good managers will gladly provide positive incentives and reluctantly, but responsibly, apply negative incentives only when absolutely necessary.

Many an employee has been perceived very differently by one manager than by another, and often the only difference is in the managers' styles and approaches. The most easily observed difference is when a manager who has related well to the employee and valued the employee's contributions is replaced by a manager who does not value the same employee's skills and contributions. This can clearly be expected to result in a decline in the employee's morale which will often be accompanied by reduced performance. Without fully understanding the concept of shared credit and shared blame, the new manager will usually take the employee to task for these consequences, and this response then magnifies the effect, resulting in a lose-lose. On the other end of the scale, a new manager who values the employee and the employee's contributions can often obtain unprecedented good performance from the employee for a definite win-win.

The most important thing to realize about this effect is that people's morale and performance correlates strongly with how the employee is perceived and treated. In fact, nearly everyone has an environment dependence. The only real difference lies in to what degree their accomplishments depend on their environment. Consequently, astute managers should strive at all times to assure that an appropriate set of incentives is provided to optimize employee performance. If this is done well, good morale is automatic.

The Expectation Trap

We all fall into this trap at times, but most people never realize that they do so. Essentially, we basically place expectations on people which they cannot meet, often based on what we believe they should be able to meet because of their position in the formal structure. This is often justified (see *Pay for Performance and Performance for Pay*) but can be a significant error anyway.

In explanation, consider going into a local fast food facility and being met by an obviously new employee wearing a tag that says "TRAINEE". If the trainee makes a mistake and miscounts your change, this is consistent with your expectations and therefore acceptable. However, you would not expect the establishment manager to miscount your change. In fact, this would not be acceptable at all, particularly if repeated. Thus, expectations are not necessarily assigned according to the individual's capabilities but according to our perception of the capabilities which are commensurate with his or her role. Because placing such expectations is done subconsciously, we all encounter situations where others fail outright to meet our expectations, and we generally fault the other party instead of revising our expectations. Clearly, a definite trap exists into which we all fall (most of us frequently) and which can only lead to disappointment. In particular, some technical and other analytical employees have a strong tendency to expect logic, reason, and rational thought to prevail at all times, and of course they cannot.

The main value of this concept is to understand the existence of the trap and the ease with which one can fall into it. Having such understanding, each person needs to try not to place unmeetable expectations on others or on oneself in the workplace.

Making Others Glad When You Win

I learned about this from a lady whose son's girlfriend persuaded him to cancel a Saturday ball game with his buddies to take her to the beach. When they returned, the mom asked the girlfriend if they had had a good day at the beach. The girlfriend had responded that they hadn't had a good day because the water was cold, sand got into everything, and the day was overcast and rainy. The mom then explained that her son would definitely go with his buddies next Saturday because the girlfriend had never learned that, when she won, she should make others glad that she did.

We each should learn to find ways to make others glad when we win. This can be extremely useful in the workplace in providing positive reinforcement for cooperation and contributions ranging from seemingly trivial to very significant, but it is not included in most managers' toolkits.

Moderating

This term is extracted from nuclear power technology. In a nuclear fission reactor, light atoms which have almost exactly the same mass as neutrons can most effectively receive energy from the neutrons that are expelled from the nucleus during fission. In essence, collisions with these light atoms cause the non-usable high-energy neutrons to become less excited and therefore more suitable for causing additional fission reactions. The material containing the light atoms is called a moderator because of the change of the neutrons from high energy to moderate energy.

As a management concept, moderating is a role in which one person helps an overly-excited coworker become less excited and hence more effective for the task at hand. I came to understand the concept at a previous job where two peers and I would alternatingly observe one another in a destructively excited state. The calmer observer would inform the excited friend that he or she needed a break and a soft drink. The observer treated and took the excited friend into a nearby conference room, and the excited friend was encouraged to vent his or her anxiety to a supportive, non-threatening listener. When the excited friend was sufficiently moderated to be highly effective, both parties returned to the workplace, usually with everyone else none the wiser.

It is of utmost importance that everyone have at least one person close at hand with whom he or she can take turns moderating as needed.

Never Wrestle With A Pig

"Never wrestle with a pig — you both get all dirty, and the pig loves it!"

(Also posted on bulletin boards at a previous workplace.)

While seemingly a silly homily, this concept can save the thoughtful manager considerable frustration and can often preserve effective work relationships which could otherwise easily be damaged or destroyed. In practice, we each have times when we are tempted to confront someone else who is not receptive and is likely to respond with vengeance. This concept means that we should assess each situation and not often engage in such confrontations. (Note: Following this advice would seem to be easy but for some of us is not!) (See *Choosing Where to Take Your Hits*.)

The Perception-Reality Gap

When this concept was first explained to me, I was still young enough to believe that most issues were cut-and-dried – at least those regarding personal values which anyone could observe for themselves. For example, everyone should be able to easily figure out who is or is not honest because truth will always come out. In my first role as a manager (much to my dismay), one of my employees completely misread me and expected me to do vindictive things which did not even occur to me. Her fear spread to others temporarily, and the overall group's morale and efficiency were negatively affected. Luckily, my manager at the time understood this concept and was willing to work through it with me.

To understand this effect, consider going into a store with only a few minutes to buy a particular item, finding the item, and then realizing that the salesperson is absent (perhaps in the restroom). After waiting as long as you can, you leave the price tag, the exact change, and a note of explanation. Seeing this, a bystander hides after taking the tag, money, and note. Then you are confronted outside the store by a security guard under suspicion of theft of the item. As you are unable to prove your innocence, the guard can only have the perception that you are a thief. In reality, you are not.

This example may seem contrived, but the effect illustrated by it happens in the workplace and can have serious consequences. So each manager must learn to consider the possibility of this perception-reality gap in dealing with employee issues and to explain its existence to others. (See *Poise vs. Reacting Based on Hearsay.*)

Perfection – (No One Can Achieve It, Good or Bad)

One of the ways to enable yourself to allow others to make mistakes is to bear in mind that no one can achieve perfection. Knowing this, you must also know that even the boss or the absolute strongest performer must make some mistakes. Also, this should certainly allow each of us to realize that we also cannot achieve perfection and must, therefore, sometimes be mistaken. This of course necessitates allowance for disagreement if our mistakes are to be caught.

The corollary to this, though, is that even the most mistake-prone or least informed person cannot accomplish being perfectly wrong or wrong every time, and we need to watch for the times when we might disagree with someone who is right just because we expect them to be wrong (as usual).

RULE #1: The boss is always right.

RULE #2: When the boss is wrong, see
rule #1.

(Originator unknown.)

Personal Sanity and Well-being: A Model of Balance

Everyone experiences good and not-so-good times at work and away from work. Some bear the bad times better than others, but everyone has limits as to how much grief they can withstand, and grief beyond these limits jeopardizes their personal sanity and general well-being. In an effort to provide a usable understanding level with the least possible complication, the following model has been developed:

First, three categories to a person's life are defined as their job or vocation; their home life (non-work interactions such as with family, friends, neighbors, etc.); and their hobbies. Over years, nearly everyone has activities in all three of these categories, and they should. The model proposes that each person's ability to sustain his or her sanity and general well-being does not depend on any one of these, but rather on a combination of the three. The combination can change such that each category can change from good to bad or from bad to good temporarily without having too large an effect. From a personal standpoint, which particular categories are going well may seem important, but the combination is the most important factor.

Among the three categories, it is a rare and fortunate individual who has all three go well for great lengths of time. However, having two go well while the third is not normally provides the person with a favorable balance and is very satisfactory. Having only one going well while two are not is unhealthy and is liable to negatively affect the person's well-being and sanity if this unfavorable balance persists too long. The worst case of course is for none of the three to be going well. This combination comprises a serious threat to sanity and well-being and definitely calls for a change.

To be effective, a manager should watch and listen to be cognizant that each employee has at least an acceptable balance according to the model. Of course, the manager should also strive at all times to help the employee have the job go well. Having his or her hobbies and home life go well is healthy for the employee, but this can actually reduce the employee's urgency to improve a bad situation at work until something goes wrong with the employee's home life or hobbies, and such a reduced urgency can then impair the employee's performance. Realizing this, the manager should seek ways to help improve the employee's job situation without simultaneously causing problems in the other categories.

In summary, the employee's personal sanity and general well-being can be expected to be sustained if things are going well for the employee in at least one, and preferably two, of the categories of job, home life, and hobbies. Since the main charter of a manager is to get work done through his or her employees, the manager should clearly most prefer that the employee has things going well at the job. However, if problems on the job are expected to be temporary but unavoidable, prudent managers will seek ways to ensure that the employee has a favorable balance among the three categories by somehow improving the employee's home life and/or hobbies. (The problem with ensuring such is that the manager frequently can only use the informal structure to avoid meddling in the employee's personal life, and sometimes the manager cannot help at all in these other categories.)

Perspective

It is a given that everyone's perspective is unique and that each person's perspective evolves through a series of events. Two events particularly stand out for me and are shared here because they have enabled me to maintain perspective for many years and have repeatedly been helpful to others.

In the first instance, I was actually one of over a hundred crew members on a submarine which hit an underwater peak while submerged and approaching North America from farther out at sea. Standing near the stern of this very large object when it suddenly pivoted about its centers of mass and buoyancy, I felt the fluttery sensation in the pit of my stomach that you normally feel when your seat suddenly drops as on a roller coaster. This was followed by scraping sounds on the hull (you couldn't tell from where) and everyone wondering what was happening. While I can't state that I felt fear, there was an immediate realization of our mortality and the lack of control of our fate which I have never forgotten. Years later, when it has been necessary to occupy a firm position, I have had others express their worry that I might incur someone's wrath or even lose a job. While these outcomes are undesirable and unpleasant, they pale in comparison to the potential loss of a boat and everyone's lives. (Note: Two submarines with friends of mine aboard did sink during my time on submarines.) Each time that I remember this, my perspective is that I am bolstered in my commitment to be counted where needed and to accept the results.

In the second instance, we were submerged for a long patrol once and then returned to port. I had only one opportunity to go to several shops in town to purchase souvenirs and other articles which I had ordered previously for my family, and it rained steadily throughout this opportunity. Because of this being the only chance to shop and not having seen the sun or breathed outside air for sixty-four consecutive days, I really could not be upset by the rain. As in the first instance, I have remembered this often (though not always) when the weather has been unpleasant, and the memory has provided me with an acceptance and comfort regardless of the weather because of the perspective it provides.

Everyone has had experiences which can be similarly applied, and the two anecdotes above are provided to stimulate thought in terms of perspective with the hope that this is helpful.

Picking Up The Calf

A farmer, finding a newborn calf in the field, can easily pick it up and carry it into the barn for warmth, shelter, and feeding. If the calf gets out of the barn the next day, the farmer can easily pick up the calf again and return it to the barn. However, the calf can later actually gain as much as several pounds in a day. Therefore, there is a particular, identifiable day when the farmer absolutely can no longer pick up the calf and knows it.

When significant growth occurs in an organization or job, the increase in difficulty to fully meet the needs can be imperceptible on a daily basis, and hence not perceived at all by the person who is trying to do the job. Over time, the job can change so much that the person is completely unable to do it. Yet the person still resists relinquishing any of the responsibilities in a vain attempt to continue "picking up the calf". This is a very common effect, but vanity prevents most managers from ever saying that they can no longer do the job (even if it has tripled in difficulty or scope).

Another way that this effect is manifested is when a manager fails to recognize that the job of an employee has grown significantly and consequently does not provide the employee with relief or help. Instead, the manager will typically expect the employee to continue "picking up the calf", perhaps even suggesting that the employee become better organized or manage his or her time more effectively (this is addressing the symptom while ignoring the cause). This indicates that the manager has clearly lost contact with the increased scope of the employee's job, and this state usually continues until the employee leaves and the manager must define the job to hire a replacement (or two, as sometimes occurs).

Picking Up Pennies

While walking back to work after lunch with a peer one day, a supervisor noticed the peer reaching down to pick up a penny from the roadway as if he had found a treasure. As a boy, the supervisor used to walk miles to pick up soft drink bottles worth 2¢ each because a candy bar or soft drink only cost 5¢. A penny was definitely worth picking up then, and over the years the supervisor's children also took delight in finding them. However, he had recently realized that a single penny would no longer buy anything consequential and actually only wears out your pocket faster. Thinking about this, the supervisor was finally able to quit stooping for the occasional penny which can no longer provide any discernible effect on his buying power.

Interestingly, the above incident occurred while a situation at work was running through the supervisor's mind. In this situation, his own management had been unwilling to authorize a $2 expense for each of a dozen engineers for work-related pamphlets. Compared to the overall expense of employing those engineers, saving the cost of these pamphlets was analogous to picking up pennies from the roadway. In fact, the time spent (debating whether to buy the pamphlets or not) cost the company several times the proposed expense and frustrated several people who had seen one of the pamphlets and considered their purchase a good idea. Not wanting to be also perceived as one who considered the employees as not being worth $2 each, the supervisor wrote a personal check for several copies and gave them to his employee group.

The reason to expend so many words on this effect is that many managers spend considerable time unprofitably looking for pennies to pick up in the workplace, and perhaps describing the effect will provide at least one such manager, current or prospective, with a better perspective so that his or her time can be better spent on "bigger stuff."

Room Size vs. Comfort/Discomfort Level

My first job as a manager was in a facility with several sizes of conference rooms, with the smallest having just enough space for two people to converse in close physical proximity. These smallest rooms were almost always available, and other managers used them for performance reviews. However, sensitive or potentially confrontational discussions in these close quarters regularly produced high employee anxiety. Realizing this after one very difficult conversation, I began to experiment by deliberately scheduling various-sized rooms. When an unpleasant discussion was held in a large room, the outcome was indisputably more constructive. Consequently, the following principle is proposed:

When planning an employer-employee discussion, the size of the room scheduled must be inversely proportional to the anticipated comfort level of the discussion.

In essence, this means that to give an employee news with which he or she will be very pleased, a tiny room can be used. But to discuss a topic which can reasonably be expected to provide the employee with displeasure or stress, a large room is needed. (I actually have taken some employees outside on a sunny day for very difficult discussions such as discussing their not getting a job for which they have strongly aspired or to try to remove anger which they held toward someone else.)

A corollary to this principle is that difficult manager-employee conversations should never be held in the manager's office because of the lack of a neutral ground. Also, such conversations should definitely be scheduled in advance and not triggered unexpectedly by an approach such as "Do you have a minute? If so, please come into my office." Such an approach sends a message that the manager considers the employee's time to be unimportant.

Scheming Positively (or Laying Pipe)

The word "scheming" is almost universally received with a negative connotation. This adds emphasis to the ability to get people to listen when explaining this concept. However, this expression can be used with a positive connotation to describe getting something done through creative thought, anticipation of potential obstacles, and careful monitoring of the progress needed to overcome the obstacles. Essentially, it is nothing more than planning, discussing your plans until you have the buy-in of the principle parties needed to effect the plans, and then making the plans come true.

As a manager, I use this as an effective tool to obtain banner performance from employees. Early in my own career, I was told that particular positive rewards were deserved but could not be delivered because they weren't provided in the budget. Considering this argument as "lame" (according to today's vernacular of the young), I decided to always try diligently to foresee rewardable events and to incorporate these in the annual budget and planning documents. For example, approval of a

71

promotion recommendation can be obtained much more easily if the recommended pay increase is reflected in the existing budget and the promotion itself is listed in the appropriate location of the annual plan. In fact, when told that a reward cannot be provided, a predictable purchase cannot be made, or a trade show or seminar cannot be attended because of not being included in the budget, my own internal response is usually "Who made up the budget without looking ahead?" Also, I don't like to leave myself vulnerable to the same question, so I try to foresee all possibilities and have appropriate contingencies in the plans.

I have heard others refer to this as "laying pipe", but I refer to it as scheming positively. Regardless of what this tactic is called, every manager should consider its use as one of the fundamental ingredients for real success. (See *Motivation Through Compacts*.)

Significant Disagreement

This concept is very helpful in achieving a consensus agreement where unanimous agreement either is unnecessary or is blocked by an unyielding minority. It is also valuable to expedite consensus agreement with minimum debate when quick resolution is needed. Quite simply, one need only state a position and call for adoption of that position unless "significant disagreement" exists. If no one expresses such disagreement, the position can be adopted and the next issue can be addressed.

Too Far Too Fast

This is a career hazard for those on the advancement "fast track." One part of the hazard is difficulty actually understanding the job levels over which the fast tracker has dominion, and another part is the lack of acceptance by peers and superiors. Some truly exceptional people can overcome these effects, but most can't. In essence, the basic effect is one by which someone advances so rapidly through promotions that they lack the skills to be accepted or marketable at the organizational level they have reached and are considered too expensive to be assigned at their actual level of competency. In fact, they often are not marketable at one or two levels of their latest positions because of not having become "established" at those levels either. As long as the person can hold onto the present position, they may actually become both competent and established at that level, but a significant risk exists for them if for some reason they can't hold on.

A good example was an individual who hired into a large company at an entry level in management and was promoted rapidly to a position essentially three levels higher in a much more technical discipline within three years. Then he was displaced and did not have sufficient experience at each of the other positions to be perceived as established at those levels. As described above, he was overpriced for the level considered most appropriate and didn't possess sufficient tenure to be considered as established at his two most recent job levels. Obtaining a new position was a serious problem for him because he had advanced too far too fast.

The YSYL Principle

(Pronounced "eissel," as in Eiffel Tower.)

This stands for "You snooze – you lose" and can often be observed when someone either is missing or late for a meeting in which undesirable assignments can reasonably be expected to be handed out. (The person missing is assigned something without being able to decline and later told "You snooze – you lose".)

Note: This is acceptable and humorous for a cohesive team with strong camaraderie and mutual respect but can be dangerous otherwise.

The Cowboy Hat – A Counterexample

A man working for a large employer was beginning his vacation when, boarding the plane in his casual clothing, he was approached by a management representative to postpone his trip and solve a significant, unexpected production problem. The manager promised the company would replace the man's travel tickets and reservations in kind, so the man agreed. Because of the urgency of the problem, he went directly to work without changing clothes and wearing an expensive cowboy hat. In the course of solving the problem, his cowboy hat was ruined, so the man included the cost of a replacement in his next expense report. However, his manager's boss would not allow reimbursement for the cowboy hat because it was not needed on the man's job normally, and he did not fully appreciate the man's having interrupted his vacation.

Seeing the futility of recovering the expense by listing it as a cowboy hat, the man was able to recover the expense by becoming much more serious about tracking small, but legitimate, business expenses and submitting these expenses for reimbursement. When the amount reimbursed for these previously unincluded expenses was sufficient, the man bought a new cowboy hat, wore it ostentatiously, and openly challenged his management to find the cowboy hat in his listed expenses (which of course could not be done).

Several basic principles come to the fore in this scenario. First, the management was obviously "picking up pennies". Second, the manager's boss did not delegate and allow the reimbursement decision to be made at the lowest appropriate level in the organization. Third, the manager's boss, with a conflict between *reason* and *rules for ordinary circumstances*, allowed the rules to prevail over reason. Lastly, the episode significantly reduced the man's loyalty to the company, and this can't easily be regained.

Tips for Strategic Managers

Chapter VI

Management Practices to Avoid

The pitfalls for managers are many. Because the opportunity to fall into these is so great, considerable thought needs to be given to carefully avoid doing so. Regrettably, each of the topics addressed in this chapter is pertinent in the modern workplace. And each can be observed much too prevalently.

These topics are presented to help managers guard against the basic errors described here. They also will probably alert some employees of managers who would use these tactics. Hopefully, this will make it more difficult for such managers to disguise efforts to deceive or to pursue the wrong priorities.

Activity Traps

Most managers, at some time or other, direct employees to complete assignments which really don't contribute to business needs. These can aptly be defined as activity traps, and are usually the result of too little thought by the manager, insufficient or inaccurate information behind the decision to make the assignment, or poorly defined business objectives. Regardless of the cause, however, activity traps expend resources which could be applied more effectively and serve as an irritant to the employee who recognizes them for what they are.

Compatible with earlier material, the employee who recognizes an activity trap should question the assignment (See *Loyalty* and *It's Okay to Disagree*). If still assigned the activity trap, the employee should accept the assignment and do the task well (See *Allowing Others to Make Mistakes*). But knowing that assignment of activity traps is altogether too easy, every manager should try not to assign them or to have them discontinued after they have been identified.

Carrying the Plant

Many managers, particularly those in new positions, consider their support staff not to be sufficiently capable or motivated to correct the problems which exist in the workplace. Such managers also feel a strong need to find solutions by themselves. While this feeling can develop quite naturally when the manager knows that the organization is substantially behind on deliveries or is not meeting expectations on the quality and costs associated with the organization's products, it also can provide very destructive results.

When a manager (or anyone else) decides that only he or she has the combined commitment and ability to prevent a disaster because of organizational non-performance, the temptation is to assume more and more responsibility for the results and to rely less and less on others. This tendency to attempt to do everything yourself can only end up in reduced contributions from others and an escalating need for the carrier to carry even more. In a manufacturing environment, this effect can easily be described as carrying the plant. Of course, no one would deliberately attempt such a thing suddenly, so the effect normally develops over time, sometimes almost imperceptibly. Some signs of carrying the plant include reluctance to delegate, longer work hours, a high frustration level, wondering why others don't care, and a sensation that no one else is able to figure out appropriate solutions.

Whenever this effect becomes evident, the carrying manager (or other person) needs to immediately formulate a strategy to enlist stronger commitment from the people who should share the burden of correcting the problems and, if necessary, provide them with increased training or tools to assure their success. This should be followed by extending trust, deliberately releasing some responsibilities through delegation, and publicizing the team's successes to maintain their new or renewed commitment and capability. (See *The Manager as Publicist*.)

Contradictions

As is indicated throughout this work, in order to get the best results from employees, a manager needs to provide clear, consistent leadership with ambitious, but attainable, goals. Failure to be consistent can be as damaging to the manager's ability to motivate employees as a lack of integrity can be. Yet some managers show no concern whatever and can provide logical contradictions on a regular basis. For example, some managers will openly discuss what should be confidential information regarding some employees while telling others not to make such disclosures. Or they will declare that disagreement is acceptable and even encouraged but then punish anyone who does disagree. The mixed messages transmitted by these and other contradictions can provide employees with tremendous confusion and cause them to expend considerable energy and time trying to figure out which message is real instead of applying these resources to their assigned work.

Understandably, no manager can be totally consistent because of being human, but inconsistency or contradiction from a manager must be highly unusual to not seriously impair effectiveness. Also, when an inconsistency is brought to the manager's attention, he or she needs to listen constructively and, if possible, make an appropriate correction. If the inconsistency or contradiction is actually a rare occurrence and is not resolvable, employees should accept this as such and go forward. (See *It's Okay to Disagree* and *Allowing Others to Make Mistakes.*) However, the main point of issue here is that some managers are only consistent in their utterance or commission of contradictions, and this is patently inexcusable.

Credit Stealing

Almost self-explanatory, this is an extremely effective way for a manager to lose employee loyalty, thereby providing the manager with no motivational tool except position power. In the short run, the manager who steals credit for employees' accomplishments (even if partial credit is due the manager) may advance his or her career, but use of this tactic on a sustained basis will result in alienation of those from whom the manager needs support the most. Consequently, the user of this tactic can expect to eventually find his or her career stifled or even destroyed. Some such managers never connect the later effect to the wrong earlier behavior, but the victims whose credit has been stolen do. (See *Shared Credit – Shared Blame*).

Discrediting Others: A Lose-Lose

Because of the importance of teamwork and the overall success of the organization as a whole, all managers should seek ways to always encourage cooperation within and across organizational lines. Contrary to this, some managers actually seem to believe in pitting themselves or their employees against others. Lacking confidence in their own ability to compete, these managers try to make themselves look good by making others look bad. Consequently, they resort to discrediting those with whom they disagree, those who they perceive as threats, and those who they perceive as politically acceptable targets. While such actions may provide the temporary illusion of at least victory over the discredited party, others in the organization are quick to catch on, and the manager's effectiveness is hence reduced not only with the target of discreditation but with others too.

The effect of this practice is a sure lose-lose regardless of the position or title of the initiator, but is most destructive for anyone in a position of authority. Nevertheless, it is a practice which can be observed in most organizations and therefore needs to be understood by us all.

Elevating the Buck

This phrase can be used to describe any of three effects. The first has to do with unwillingness to take risk, the second with trying to avoid blame, and the third with a desire to unload a problem performer.

For the first effect, consider a situation in which a decision is needed and the manager responsible for the outcome considers the logical choice to potentially be controversial or exceedingly unpopular. Lacking the courage to have his or her name connected to the controversy, the manager then defers the decision to his or her own manager, thus avoiding blame for any undesirable outcomes. (Note that the deferring manager has also avoided receiving credit for controversial decisions which have favorable outcomes and misses the opportunity to learn from success or failure related to risk.) Such a manager is perhaps an administrator but clearly not a leader—and should step down.

For the second effect, consider a manager in whose department a strong negative event has occurred (a schedule missed, a budget overrun badly, an incorrect process used which resulted in ruined product, etc.). A weak manager will want to blame someone else – however that can be done. If it is determined that the problem resulted from a management decision and not from employee error, this manager will try to pass the blame to his or her superiors, essentially projecting a posture of impotence in the decision-making process. This clearly demonstrates that the manager in question either does not understand several of the concepts presented elsewhere in this manuscript (See *Shared Credit – Shared Blame, Allowing Others to Make Mistakes*, and *What's The Best Thing To Do Now?*) or operates only from a base of misplaced self-interest. Among other things, this effect transmits a lack of team spirit, a lack of loyalty to superiors, and a strong personal insecurity in the participating manager. The damage from these messages can be expected to be greater than the consequences of nearly any triggering negative event.

For the third effect, consider a manager who has an employee with whom the manager has discomfort but who is sufficiently entrenched politically to preclude demotion or dismissal. In self-interest, the manager successfully recommends the employee for promotion in another organization. Thus, the manager's source of discomfort is removed, and the overall organization has a new person in an unearned leadership role. This third effect is as bad as the first two.

The End-of-the-Month Spike

In many workplaces, the work to be completed daily varies greatly during the month, usually according to a repeated pattern. Managers usually have some ready explanation for this effect involving external customers, system problems, availability of materials, or other uncontrollable causes. The effect usually is fully evident on a monthly cycle but can also show up semiannually or annually. Of course, some of the causes given in explanation are usually real if other factors are ignored, and the manager who decides to eliminate these periodic spikes will be met with impassioned statements regarding the impossibility of the task.

However, the ability to smooth the daily work requirements normally only depends on the commitment to do so and the ability of the manager to make a better plan. This seems easy to say and difficult to accomplish, but by identifying the actual causes and taking corrective action for each, significant improvement can be achieved. For example, if a system problem is a legitimate cause, then the system must be improved. Similarly, if the availability of materials is a legitimate cause, then an improved method of planning and procuring materials must be developed. And once corrective actions have been taken, a mindset must be developed through which uneven daily workloads are not acceptable without truly extraordinary causes. When such extraordinary causes exist, then managers must accept the results. But not on a routine and periodic basis.

In fact, in most instances, the work can be planned so that, by the work required, the last day of the month or the last week of a fiscal year will not be distiguishable from any other day or week. This enables employees to do their best at all times, including final days when no time is left for recovery from mistakes.

The End Run

This can be one of the most destructive practices of all in the workplace. Essentially, it consists of any employee (at any level in the organization) going to his or her boss's boss with a complaint or request but without having first provided his or her boss the opportunity to address the issue at hand. On the assumption that either the employee's boss has had such an opportunity or that addressing the issue will boost their own image as being accessible and supportive, many of the boss's bosses forget fundamental principles and make agreements which should actually be relegated to the employee's boss. Regardless of the correctness or error of the agreement, such action undermines the effectiveness of the employee's own boss and encourages the particular employee (and others) to continue the process. This also results in the boss's boss having to expend exorbitant time to issues which should be delegated, thereby reducing the time available for his or her own proper responsibilities.

Each manager who is approached by someone who works for someone else below the approached manager in the organization should, as a first step, check to assure that each appropriate intermediate person has had an opportunity to address the issue. If this has occurred, the manager can ethically proceed. However, if this has not occurred, the approached manager needs to send the employee back to the appropriate person to prevent the complications which nearly always result from the end run.

The converse effect, by which a manager bypasses a subordinate and gives direction to or makes agreement with the subordinate's employees, on his or her own volition and without the subordinate's knowledge, also constitutes an end run and is equally destructive.

Flag-in-the-Wind Management

Just as a flag has no defined direction but will turn in whatever direction to which the wind shifts it, some managers are willing to alter their direction at any moment based on whim. Usually these managers are either seriously insecure, dedicated followers, or both. Employees of these managers, though, don't know what to expect from day to day and are thus unable to plan and achieve long-term objectives. While the managers who exhibit this behavior *should* be held accountable for their actions, they usually are themselves victims of management without defined long-range goals. Because of this, they don't typically consider themselves accountable. Nevertheless, this effect is extremely destructive to morale and business performance.

The Knighthood System

Many managers who need to hire a subordinate manager believe that their best performer will automatically make the best manager. This idea has particular absurdity in some disciplines because of the dissimilarity of the skills for the manager assignment and the manager's subordinate's assignments. For example, the skills essential to excel as a typist, accountant, or electronic circuit designer don't coincide with those needed to motivate employees, to develop and monitor budgets, and for other responsibilities of management.

In too many organizations, people are rewarded for their performance at their assigned tasks until the only remaining reward is to promote them out of their skill base by "knighting" them as managers. The results of this usually are reduced group performance because of the loss of a strong performer at the assigned task and poor leadership because of an unqualified manager. The "knighted" appointee often is also unhappy because of the frustration of not being able to provide performance at the previous stellar level. However, if the "knighted" person works for someone who also was previously knighted, the newly-appointed person usually receives strong positive reinforcement for inadequate performance in the new role because the appointee doesn't know better either.

The viable alternatives to the knighthood system are other rewards for non-managerial performance, methodical development of the strong performers for management, and increased pay and titles for exceptional performers. Regardless of the alternative chosen, the knighthood system is a type of designed failure, though this may not be recognized for a long time.

Management By Negative Surprise

Some managers are exceedingly reluctant to provide negative feedback, either because of a lack of courage or a lack of candor. Because of this, such a manager often will regularly tell an employee that his or her performance is acceptable or better until the time comes for a written appraisal of the employee's performance. Or the manager will fail to discuss issues with the employee and let them accumulate until delivering a long, and mostly outdated, agenda. Meanwhile in either case, the employee will have continued to perform at a stable level, under the justified belief that this is the desired performance level. Until the moment of the negative surprise! When the manager finally confronts the employee, the effect provides anger and alienation which impairs improvement of the performance in question as well as a loss of trust.

In one case of this, a manager would become angry over something and provide retaliatory disciplinary documentation in which performance previously evaluated as good was retroactively discredited and evaluated as unsatisfactory. In order to generate the retaliatory documentation, the manager would actually engage in what has historically been referred to as muckraking by soliciting negative inputs from peers and subordinates of the target of his anger. When muckraking, the manager discounted positive reports and asked pointedly for negative reports to demean his target. Such a process is unacceptable and results in complete elimination of a manager's ability to motivate employees. (See *Integrity*.)

For a better way to be effective as a manager, performance discussions should be held on an ongoing basis with openness and candor so that significant events, whether positive or negative, are not surprises to the employee. Employees entering performance discussions should know basically what the outcome will be and only have questions regarding the details. Yet some managers manage by negative surprise despite even having received training against such behavior. This is one of the worst behaviors a manager can exhibit. (See *Room Size vs. Comfort/Discomfort*

Level and *Motivation Through Compacts.*)

Meddling

Contrary to other discussions about extending trust, delegation, and allowing others to make mistakes, many managers cannot resist trying to direct every activity and decision of their employees. This behavior tells the employees that the manager has no confidence in anyone else. Even if the employees are fully incapable (which usually is not even close to true), the manager has his or her own job to do and cannot do that job *and* those of the employees. Thus, the net results of meddling by the manager are reduced morale, increased backlog, fatigue, and loss of acceptance by the manager's employees – not a good combination.

Please note that each manager has both a right and an obligation to be informed and helpful regarding each employee's work, but the point of issue here is the degree of involvement. Basically, the manager should direct employee efforts at the top level and leave the details to the employees except in rare instances. (See *Delegation.*) Otherwise, the manager should step down to the employee job level.

The Moving Carrot Trick

This is a tactic by which rewards are promised for particular accomplishments or at particular service intervals, withheld, and then promised again. Of course, the promisor will always contend somehow that failure to deliver the reward is justified, and often this trick can work effectively as a one-time, short-term motivator. But, repeated, it can only lead to distrust and a loss of loyalty. (See *Honoring Promises.*)

In a most notable and extreme case of this effect, a new engineer was told to expect a raise with a three-month review. But after three months, he was told that there hadn't been enough time for sufficiently measurable results, and the raise was being deferred until his six-month review. The six month review was held late, at eight months, and he was told that a raise was justified but that a larger raise could be awarded at the one-year interval (in June) if he would wait. Almost predictably, at one year, a factor completely beyond his control temporarily caused what looked like poor results from him, and he was told that no raise was justified. His manager later realized that the cause of the poor results at the time of the one-year review had not been within the engineer's control and told the engineer that the review cycle was being revised to an August/February system with half of the engineers' reviews in each. He then promised that if the results were good by August, the engineer would receive the long-awaited raise. All goals were met in July and August, but the engineer was told that his June review was too recent and that his next review would now slip to February. This final move of the carrot propelled the engineer to accept a promotion and significant raise to leave (which was offered because of knowledge of others of the actual results obtained).

Of course, there are many ways to administer (or more accurately *withhold*) the moving carrot, and the results are completely predictable. As is indicated in *The Paid Trip*, the main difference between people who leave jobs and people who stay is that the leavers are under-rewarded. Hence, use of the moving carrot trick can be expected inevitably to result in increased employee turnover.

The New Corporal Effect

At a private high school with a military training program and an excellent academic program, it was obvious even to new sophomores that some people, given their first opportunity to do so, begin issuing arbitrary orders as a show of authority. At the school, the first such opportunity accompanied promotion to the rank of corporal. Thus, over the years, the students learned to watch with humor the actions of new corporals after each time that promotions were posted. While the effect wasn't limited to corporals, it was most visibly demonstrated by them.

Sadly, this effect also occurs just as clearly in many instances when people are promoted to supervisory or management positions. Also, recovery from the accompanying syndrome is not necessarily quick or limited to the first promotion. And the worst feature of it is that the need to posture, flex, and capriciously show authority usually leads to rules prevailing over reason, and it is not humorous to have business results impaired by such behavior. The effect is a trap into which anyone can easily fall, though, so all managers should think about this effect and strive to avoid it. Managers should also caution newly-promoted subordinates to be mindful of this effect and avoid it.

Sham Interviews

These are interviews in which the basic intent is to deceive the interviewee by pretending that said interviewee is actually a candidate for a promotion or job opening when he or she, in truth, is not being seriously considered. Such an interview is a sham!

This is one of the most insulting practices available to a manager, but sham interviews are held by some managers regardless. Some motivation for this exists when organizational policies require interviewing a minimum number of candidates or perhaps all internal candidates. Some motivation also exists when the interviewing manager has an employee-candidate who will be offended to realize that he or she is considered unworthy for a desired position. Nevertheless, the sham interview wastes the time of both the interviewer and the interviewee and can, if undetected, provide false hope in the supposed candidate. If detected, it sends a message that the interviewer believes the interviewee not to be smart enough to see through the sham. While the interviewer may actually get away with this occasionally, *most* employees will either figure out for themselves that the interview was a sham or be told that by others.

Were we to disregard morality for the sake of this discussion only, the benefits possibly available from the sham interview when the ruse works don't nearly equal the consequences that can be expected when it doesn't work. However, the morality and character of managers need to be of the highest order. (See *Integrity*.) Thus, *no* argument exists for holding the sham interview except a manager's personal unwillingness or inability to tell the hopeful applicant that he or she actually is not in contention, and this argument is not viable. While declining to hold an interview may seem to be mean to the hopeful applicant, it is actually nicer than implying that the applicant isn't smart enough to see through the charade. In short, the sham interview is wrong and should never be held. In the cases where policies require interviews despite the competitiveness of the applicants, the policies need to be changed. (See *When Reason and Rules Conflict.*)

"I may have been born at night, but it wasn't last night."
Ron Wardlow

Three Confrontational Practices

Each manager has need to handle stress, and the way they do can increase or defray the allegiance of their employees. The manager who can exhibit poise and channel the energy which results from stress to constructive efforts will receive respect and loyalty. Unfortunately, not all managers can do this, so the following descriptions of destructive behaviors are presented as counter examples.

1. Fireside Chats:

A manager was notorious for transferring stress to the employee base by calling people into the manager's office unexpectedly and asking them to close the door. This was invariably followed by conversation in which the manager would dole out blame for some stressful event. In those conversations, blame might be assigned by the manager to the employee, the manager's boss, or any other available target, but was never accepted by the manager. (See *Shared Credit-Shared Blame.*) This manager would pose as a very caring individual who was concerned for the employee's welfare and would encourage the employee not to repeat or adopt the behavior which led to the event. Because of the pretext

91

that the manager tried to pose as a friend while usually providing serious negative reinforcement (deserved or undeserved) to the employee, this scenario is described as a series of fireside chats. Regardless of terminology, this practice is an irritant to employees and impairs a manager's effectiveness.

2. The White-Knuckle Effect:

Another manager who inherited a department in severe disarray faced nearly impossible demands for the manager and the employee base to meet. The combination of the enormity of the tasks at hand and the commitment of the manager produced severe stress for the manager who typically exhibited admirable composure and poise. However, on occasion, the stress would be too great and the manager, instead of taking quiet time or otherwise relieving the stress, would vent the stress on a subordinate. In these instances, the manager would point one finger, wave it vigorously, and clinch the other fingers so tightly that all of the knuckles on the hand with the pointed finger would be almost as white as ivory. During these white-knuckle confrontations, the manager would strive to intimidate the subordinate. However, because the subordinates recognized this as unusual, stress-induced behavior, their most frequent response was compassion. The risk associated with these events was very high, however, and behavior like this can be expected to be catastrophic for most managers.

3. Publicly Confronting an Individual's Mistake:

Some managers believe this to be a viable strategy, but it can instead provide embarrassment and divide the manager's team. In one notable example, a manager had a subordinate inform his peers about a business trip. This went well until the employee revealed that he had spent approximately triple the normal amount for breakfast in the hotel (supposedly to assure being at a seminar session at the starting time). The manager then scolded the employee in particular and the group in general in an effort to instill commitment by everyone to guard the till. The manager's main error was in implying that the other employees would also have bought the expensive breakfast instead of managing their time better and going across the street for a less expensive breakfast. All of the other employees in the meeting were annoyed and irritated, and each expressed later that the discussion about the price of breakfast should have been held in private. (Please note too that this "extra" expense was approximately two per cent of the trip expense. (See *Perspective* and *Picking Up Pennies*.) Of course, the public manager-employee confrontation over a disagreement between the employee and someone else is just as destructive.

In summary, there are too many destructive confrontational practices available to describe them all here, but hopefully the examples given can alert concerned managers to some of the dangers of such practices. If even one manager can apply this idea and avoid or discontinue such a practice, the effort documenting these will have been worthwhile.

Withholding Rewards

In an earlier topic, the successful approach of motivating employees through compacts was discussed. However, the key to success in this approach is the *delivery* of the promised rewards. Such delivery gives credence to future compacts. Failure to deliver, however, clearly demotivates employees and leads to increased turnover.

One explanation sometimes given for withholding rewards is the need to hold the line on expenses. In the short term, this might make sense on the one hand, but recruitment and training of replacements for disenchanted employees is almost always more costly than the withheld reward would have been. And quantification of the cost of reduced productivity because of demotivation of employees who don't leave is impossible. **One thing is certain: Withholding rewards is an ineffective management practice.** (See *Honoring Promises*, *Integrity*, and *The Moving Carrot Trick*.)

The "Yeah, Sure." Effect

Many people want to project the image of being "nice" in the belief that it will ingratiate employees and others while mistakenly failing to realize the importance of honoring promises. Some people become particularly prone to providing quick agreement with no actual intent to follow through. In fact, they develop such a habit of this that their response, however actually worded, can accurately be translated as "Yeah, sure." Of course, the result of this habit is a clear loss of trust followed by a loss of allegiance, and the ability of the "nice" person to motivate the recipients of such flippant assurances goes straight down the drain.

Chapter VII

Other Fundamental "Stuff"

How do you want to be remembered? How will you be remembered? How do people describe you? What criteria will assure hiring the best candidates? Which act will you follow (an easy one or a hard one)? Who's more valuable between employees who work at a steady pace and those who work in bursts?

These questions and more are addressed in this chapter with its collection of topics that don't fit conveniently into the other chapter groupings. However, the thoughts behind the topics in this chapter can be extremely helpful for the successful manager.

Constructive Laziness

This is a concept which I encountered both as a student and as a professor, particularly in mathematics courses. In essence, the idea is that if there is more than one way to solve a problem or achieve an objective, one should know each viable method, compare on a case-by-case basis, and choose the easiest effective method. Or in repetitive tasks, one should eliminate as much of the redundancy as possible, saving time, energy, and concentration for the non-repetitive tasks. On a broader scale, this concept can be compared to learning stroke savers and using macros on computer software applications or to having sequential numbers and part of the year pre-printed on personal bank checks. (Why don't they print the comma before the year on these?)

As a counter-example, in one course I have taught several times, some problems can be solved by three techniques. On tests in this course, I require that one problem be solved three times, using each technique once. Some students, seeing their first two solutions don't match, will rework the problem using these first two techniques without trying the third technique yet. Of course, students who are constructively lazy will go ahead and solve the problem by the third technique, hoping that the third solution will match one of the other two and show which solution contains an error. (The one who made me feel sad was the student who had three solutions which didn't match and still thought he had done well on the test.)

In summary, whenever something can be done correctly by the easiest approach, that should occur. However, when the easy approach fails, one needs to know how to complete the task using whatever method is needed. Trying only to use the easy approach is mere laziness and is unacceptable. Knowing when the easy approach is appropriate and then using it is *constructive* laziness and is encouraged.

The Curse of Intelligence

In many work environments, some people in positions of authority lack the integrity they should have, and try to develop advantages for themselves through sneaky or deceptive practices. These practices can often go undetected and hence be effective. However, these particular players of deception usually are clever enough to quickly determine who is most likely to see through their deception and will carefully watch them for signs of detection. As a result, being sufficiently intelligent to catch the deceivers can lead to being viewed as an adversary without ever even speaking. In one such set of circumstances, the detecting individual's eyes were watched by the deceivers for signs of recognition, so the detector could not even conceal his knowledge by remaining silent and still.

This ability to readily recognize deception and then be identified as the adversary of deceivers through involuntary responses (a flick of the eye, a furrowed brow, or other body language), I define as the curse of intelligence. Intelligence also contributes to the *Curse of Duty* described earlier.

Delegation

Each manager needs not only to accept responsibility for his or her employees' results as much as his or her own, but to also develop future managers. This latter cannot be accomplished without delegating decisions and risks to one's employees. Many managers perceive this to mean giving assignments which are well within the employees' capabilities and that the responsibility can be reclaimed at any time that the manager's comfort level declines.

What such managers don't understand is that delegation is the most significant tool at their disposal for developing star performers and future managers and must be provided earnestly with revocation occurring only in extremely rare cases. This means that the manager needs to delegate assignments which challenge the employees enough that they may fail (see *Stretch Objectives vs. "Safety."*) It also means that the manager must maintain enough poise to not interfere with the assignment when the employee makes decisions which don't coincide with those that the manager would make. Of course, the manager still has the rightful prerogative to discuss these decisions as an advisor and mentor, but revoking employee decisions sends many negative messages (lack of trust, loss of opportunity for employee growth, inability to let go, etc.) Even the most delegatory manager will at some time actually need to intercede, but this should be done only as a true last resort.

A Hiring Criteria Model

Who among us has not been offended to be told that we lack the main attribute being sought from candidates for some job opening? Particularly if the attribute is experience, who hasn't wanted to ask in retort, "Who messed up and gave you your first job?" Well, such screening exemplifies the fallacy of one-parameter decision-making. So, as a manager, how do you select the best candidate for your opening? There is, of course, no one best way to do this (explained later). But the following model is helpful and can increase the percentage of good selections.

The attribute to consider separately is work ethic, and this one is a go/no-go. If a person lacks a good work ethic, for the types of jobs for which I have done hiring, that person will not perform well.

The other three attributes are more difficult both to define and to measure, and any candidate who has the strongest combination of the three can do the job well. These are native intellect, preparation, and relevant experience. Working definitions of these are:

1) *Native Intellect* – Considered intelligence by some, this is whatever provides one with that quickness of mind that registers in the eyes when ideas flow. We all know that some people are able to think and

learn more quickly than some others. This ability is an indeniable advantage in the workplace.

2) *Preparation* – This can be a combination of formal education, special seminars, personal reading, or possibly other sources, but it mainly consists of an accumulation of background information which can be applied to the job.

3) *Relevant experience* – Almost self-explanatory, the important part of this attribute is *relevant*. This is perhaps the least important of these three attributes yet is often considered to be the most important.

Now, to understand the model, consider anyone who can perform satisfactorily in their assigned job and who exhibits a good work ethic. That person could do better yet if given a booster shot of any of the three italicized attributes. (Of course, no such booster shots exist.) Yet, with strength in any two of these, most people can perform well in most assignments through

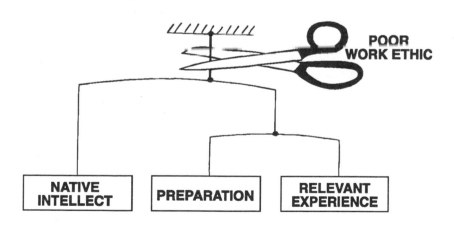

A Hiring Criteria Model

a desire to succeed. In fact, the best performance may well be available from someone with limited experience or preparation. Perhaps native intellect is the most important of these three attributes, but even that is not clear-cut, and it is the most difficult to accurately measure anyway. So the point of emphasis here is that none of the three can stand alone as a predictor of performance. Rather, as stated earlier, a suitable combination of strength in the three is what's needed to provide strong performance, and the challenge for the interviewer is to determine which candidate possesses the strongest combination.

An interesting corollary to this model is that for employee career growth, use of the hiring criteria model also provides a means for setting improvement goals. Alert managers continually seek ways to better equip their strong performers for the future, and discussion of this model provides a comfortable introduction to setting such goals, particularly for increasing an employee's preparation and relevant experience for the present job and for future career opportunities.

Isolation Factor of Promotional Success

A bright, energetic engineer was promoted to manage the group he was in. As a new manager, he emphasized strongly to his employees that he wanted them to work "with him" as compared to "for him." A very good manager, he was personable and very concerned about the people who worked with him both as employees and as support personnel (i.e. lab technicians and machinists who turned the group's designs into products). He also was a team player who applied good fundamental motivation and delegation skills.

Over the next several years, the bright, energetic man received multiple promotions (which were earned) and consequently had daily contact with a completely different set of people (usually middle and top managers). In what seemed to be a natural progression, he became isolated from the very people about whom he was so concerned earlier, exhibited increasingly transparent political behavior, and appeared to adopt values which were not acceptable to him earlier (at times seeming to be only concerned with his own success). Thus, his promotional success led to a much more aristocratic management style and a major loss of support among people he had "forgotten." Eventually, he seemed to consider people too far below him in the organizational structure as "nonpersons" and to exhibit an air of superiority which impaired his ability to retain their allegiance (which had contributed so strongly to his earlier success).

What happened in the case of this bright, energetic man does not always accompany promotional success. But his case is not particularly unusual either. Remembering that the cash flow of each company is generated through delivery of products and/or services, each manager should strive to maintain appreciation and respect for those contributors whose efforts provide this cash flow. This is difficult, though, because of the need to properly delegate and support those others who now manage those contributors. (See *The End Run* and *Delegation.*) Regardless, each manager should at least be aware of this isolation factor of promotional success and try not to let it overly hinder his or her values and effectiveness.

The Kind of Problem You Want to Have

This seems self-explanatory but still is helpful to understand. For example, if automobiles never broke down, there would be no need for automobile repairmen. And if you owned an automobile repair shop, you would ideally want to have exactly the amount of repair work to do that your staff could handle. In the real world, however, you can expect that you either have too little or too much work for a standard schedule for your staff. Between these, the problem you want to have is to figure out how to work around too much work or to turn some work away.

Quite often in the workplace, we are presented with problems which can be classified in this category. Yet many managers fail to recognize this common effect. Each needs to know that every event has consequences, positive or negative, and that if no problems existed, many of us would be completely unnecessary.

We should not generate any artificial problems but we should appreciate having those that belong to the preferable set. For example, in some situations, a customer will offer additional profitable business if aggressive timelines can be met. In such situations, the aggressive timelines are viewed as problematic, but this problem can be clearly better to have than the one of not receiving the added business. Hence this constitutes a problem of the kind that you want to have.

Managing Uphill

Just as mentoring is often mistakenly considered only a directionally downward effect, the basic effects of management are thought to be effective only downward in the organizational structure.

However, the need to get results from others is not limited to getting them only from subordinates. Everyone needs support and help sometime from others who are lateral or higher on the organizational structure, and getting work from these others is certainly a management role. Also, employees must often use persuasion to motivate their managers to follow the priorities recognized as needs by the employees. Clearly position power is not available to the subordinate employee, so reason and logic must be applied. Thus, a need exists to manage uphill as well as downhill, though managing uphill is not easy with some managers. Regardless, this is a skill which needs to be developed and applied carefully by all managers. Their own managers will value this when they recognize it if they are seasoned, quality managers themselves. (See *Loyalty*, *Mentoring*, and *Delegation*.)

One-Best-Way vs. Situational Management

At first consideration, one-best-way and situational management tend to respectively denote strength vs. weakness, certainty vs. uncertainty, pragmatism vs. idealism, etc. This is deceiving.

Actually, the manager who believes that there is always one best way is dealing strongly from idealism and has seriously weakened his or her ability to find creative solutions and approaches. In a dynamic environment, the effective manager will continually face new situations which, while often related to them, seldom are exact repetitions of old problems. This is not to say that fundamentals should be abandoned for the sake of always trying to do something new. The same fundamentals apply and can often be adapted.

Situational management is hereby defined as the application of an overall approach through which the manager considers several alternatives and the anticipated outcomes — then picks an alternative. Of course, if this choice doesn't lead to the anticipated outcome, the situational manager merely has a new decision to make for a re-start. Because of the opportunity that the situational approach provides for reason and logic to prevail, the success rate percentage is increased, and so is the manager's perceived performance. This automatically provides the situational manager with a reputation for strength, pragmatism, and certainty regarding what he or she is trying to accomplish.

One glaring example of the application of situational management is provided by baseball. In tight games, managers change pitchers or batters for left-handedness or right-handedness depending on their opponent. Occasionally, both teams will unknowingly substitute at the same time trying to gain an advantage in this attribute, and then one of them will substitute again. I once saw two consecutive players substituted as batters who never had a pitch thrown to them because the other team's pitcher substitutions iteratively changed the situation. This was, of course, a logical extreme, and no equivalent circumstance normally faces managers outside of sports.

In conclusion, the main legacy from the dean of the business school I attended is the understanding that no one-best-way exists and that all competent managers need to be situational managers. Seasoned managers find this to be true.

Providing a Quality Product in a Timely Manner at Minimum Cost

During the past twenty years, manufacturing companies have subscribed to a series of method-of-the-time programs, most with catchy acronyms, to improve their bottom lines. Some example programs are Material Requirements Planning (MRP), Statistical Process Control (SPC), Just-In-Time Manufacturing (JIT), and Management by Objectives (MBO). These have typically been promoted by management with great fanfare and official-looking memos to all employees from clusters of people with impressive titles who often are completely unknown to the recipients of the memos. These memos have been intended to lend authenticity to the current program and to inspire the labor force to make the program succeed. Yet, even with the apparent, or alleged, support of top management, these programs often fail.

The problem with subscribing to these programs does not lie in the programs themselves. Each program has been promoted because it has been successful somewhere under some set of conditions. But each program mainly focuses on only one aspect of the business, and often the set of conditions which help make it successful do not exist in the new subscribing company. Also, the method by which the programs are promoted often insults and alienates the very people who could make the programs succeed. (See *Values – Stated vs Projected vs Actual*).

What is actually needed is for the entire employee base to have a vested interest in the success of the business and to understand the following:

The real purpose in manufacturing is to provide a quality product in a timely manner at minimum cost.

Sprinters vs. Plodders

This model was developed originally while I was teaching mathematics. Two of us taught the same classes during the same quarters, but our personalities and styles were very different. My colleague was a highly competent, experienced teacher who also was very methodical and always proceeded at a steady, measured pace. I, on the other hand, frequently allowed myself to be interrupted by students' questions and told some joke or jokes in nearly every class. One student who had earlier had successive prerequisite courses taught by each of us asked me one day how I could cover as much material as my colleague when he never took time for jokes or the interruptions like I did. As we discussed his question, he stated that both approaches had resulted in his being fully prepared for the next course, and I explained that I usually sprinted through parts of the subject material. However, I also explained that most people cannot sustain the sprint (physically or mentally) and need the opportunity to regain their energy and that I was providing that opportunity with the interruptions and jokes. He then acknowledged that he had actually observed this.

In track, world-class sprinters are not suited to distance running, and the converse is just as true. Yet to win a dual meet, both types of runners are needed to accumulate the larger total of points. In the workplace, without any negative connotation intended, I refer to this as the difference between sprinters and plodders.

Given enough employees, every manager will encounter both sprinters and plodders. While sprinting is perceived as extremely valuable in urgent situations, subsequent resting in the workplace is not at all understood by or acceptable to some managers. These managers typically provide stronger rewards to plodders because they have a sustained comfort level with the plodder's efforts. This can be a major mistake in every business. (See *Focusing on What it Looks Like Someone is Doing Instead of What is Getting Done.*)

The main point to understand is that both sprinters and plodders can be valuable to the organization, and it is the manager's job (just like the track coach's) to assign people to the correct tasks so that they will be the most effective and to then reward them equitably based on their total contribution, whether it be provided in spurts or on a steady, regulated basis.

The Tail Wagging the Dog

This effect has many facets to it, as have many others. In general, though, this is defined as any situation where authority resides in the wrong hands and is applied to the detriment of business performance.

One example is for a manager to have a strong need for a purchased item to meet business objectives and pre-approved available budget for the purchase but to have the needed purchase denied by an accounting clerk who is trying to gain credit by minimizing expenditures. This sort of syndrome can result in late processing of a purchase order which then necessitates additional freight charges for expedited delivery, thus increasing expenditures.

Another example is where a person who is chartered to assure that a product meets contractual terms can, through confrontation, actually require changes to a compliant product so that it will now exceed the contractual requirements to meet the unilaterally- imposed requirements of the chartered person. This is almost always accompanied by an unwarranted added expense.

Many other examples could be listed, but for the sake of brevity, let me merely state that the tail often wags the dog, and alert managers will curtail this effect whenever they discover it.

Three Hows

The three particular questions contained in this section can be very important to a manager. How important the manager considers these questions and their answers can affect his or her effectiveness considerably. For simplicity and concision, brief answers should be considered. The questions are:

1) How do you *want* to be remembered?

The answer to this should be considered in terms such as leader, thinker, mentor, innovator, fair, supportive, etc. One colleague declared openly that if he could be known for nothing else, he wanted to be known as a thinker. As for me, I hope to be remembered as a team player and a motivator who (though strong- willed) is always susceptible to reason. This question should be answered by the individual after careful consideration. The answer can greatly help the manager to set personal goals and pursue self-improvement.

2) How *will* you be remembered?

The answer to this second question needs to be provided by others but is found through careful listening and observation. Since not everyone is candid, particularly in describing the boss to him or her because of potential perceived risk. But they cannot always hide their feelings, so an observant manager can determine their perceptions from their body language, comfort levels, and other mannerisms. Or the manager who has established a non-threatening basis of trust can get candid information from a confidante. This information must, of course, not be used incorrectly. However, the actual answers to this question provide effective feedback regarding the manager's progress toward the personal goals and self-improvement objectives from the first question.

3) How do people describe you?

As a manager, I have encountered several people who are consistently described by others with the same brief phrases or words. Two noteworthy examples were a longstanding engineer and manager who was commonly referred to as "a real gentleman" (and he was), and another engineer who was described by nearly everyone as "a very nice man" (also true). On the other hand, one manager was described by at least a dozen people from several business groups with the same expletive (and this too was accurate).

In conclusion, these questions will seem trite to some readers, and their importance doesn't lie in the particular answers, but rather in how each of us deals with the thought behind the questions. With proper consideration, these questions can be very beneficial for a manager's success.

Trigger Clauses

These are clauses included in a plan or agreement which are designed to result in an automatic progression to a next action or set of actions. Particularly useful in a status report or in the minutes from a meeting, these can document agreements for contingency plans or for sustaining the momentum of a project. Essentially, these are clauses which state that if or when some event happens, then a next event is to occur automatically. For example, if one hasn't enough money to pay the rent but is expecting a paycheck, the appropriate trigger clause might say that agreement was reached that as soon as the paycheck is received, this would trigger the actions of cashing the check and paying the rent due.

One reason to emphasize this concept is to encourage the use of trigger clauses to document agreement (or lack of significant disagreement) on planned, sequenced events and to offset use of the "Yeah Sure!" effect. (See *Significant Disagreement* and *The "Yeah, Sure!" Effect.*)

Which Act Will You Follow?

The answer to this question can be important to establishing strategies to pursue in a new assignment. Essentially, when replacing someone who previously held a position, the ease or difficulty by which one receives acceptance and support from others depends greatly on how the predecessor was perceived.

Consider a situation in which the predecessor was, for whatever reason, unpopular and ineffective. Whoever replaces this predecessor will be received with hope and optimism. Consequently, the newcomer will be supported and provided with tolerance for mistakes, particularly during the first few weeks. This is a situation in which the newcomer has an easy act to follow and is especially beneficial to a novice. Also, this situation typically accords the newcomer considerable latitude because a clear need for change exists and is recognized.

Next consider a situation in which the predecessor was respected and very effective (probably through preparation, intellect, and experience). Whoever replaces this predecessor will be compared to this role model and expected to be a stellar performer right away. (See *The Expectation Trap.*) This is definitely a hard act to follow and will require considerable caution initially regarding implementing change because of the old homily — Don't fix it if it ain't broke! This need for caution reduces the opportunity to demonstrate improvement and consequently delays (but does not preclude) acceptance for the newcomer.

As in the section entitled *Three Hows*, the value of this question lies not in the answer but in careful consideration of the question. Success and failure are both available whether the newcomer has a hard act or an easy act to follow. But responding incorrectly because of a failure to understand the question can reduce the likelihood of success.

Winning a Disproportionate Share

Some managers, particularly new ones, believe that they must win every battle or lose face each time that they lose. Actually, no one can always win. In fact, in baseball, the World Series is decided by the first team to win four games out of a possible seven. Professional basketball also allows for multiple losses with the eventual championship still available. Why then should we consider a single failure by a manager to prevail or "win" as catastrophic?

Realizing this in my second management job, I had an employee describe my first contest of wills with another department as "unwinnable" because of the other department's obstinacy and political clout. My response was that I intended to develop a strategy (see *Scheming Positively*) by which I could provide a win-win while attaining my objective but that this might in fact *be* unwinnable. However, I asked the employee to observe me over several such circumstances and told her that even though no one can always win, she would probably see me win a disproportionate share of the time. This, in my view, is the best that a manager can expect. Approximately a year later, the employee confirmed that this concept had proven to be valuable.

In order to win a disproportionate share, a manager must always consider what most benefits the overall organization, what his or her adversaries would lose, and how best to provide those adversaries with some other resultant win. The manager also must not gloat, but needs instead to strive, whenever possible, to make those adversaries glad that he or she has won. (See *Making Others Glad When you Win.*) However, it should be understood that every employee values working for a manager who is able to win when needed.

EPILOGUE

Compilation of this material has required reviewing many years of memories, and numerous people stand out because of their inspiration. In particular, my thanks go to Connie Chapman, Mark Howes, Jerry Loe, and Stan Prier for their mentoring and support. People who stand out for urging me to undertake this project include Dale Cheatham, Debbie Shintaku, Jack Hall, and Phil Johansen. Special thanks go to my wife Ardyce for all of her help typing and to my daughter Angie Tobin for her illustrations. Special thanks also go to Angie, Ann Samuelson, and Ann Phelps for test reading and editing support.

It is important to reiterate, though, that the main intent has been to share numerous constructive ideas which have been gleaned from other people, personal experiences, and observation. In particular, management is a very serious role which needs inspirational leaders with the highest integrity and sense of community. Those who have the ability to lead correctly need to accept this responsibility, prepare themselves through education and training, and continuously strive to improve (remembering all the while that one never can learn it all). If the right people either fail to accept the responsibility or to honor the commitment, the whole world is the worse for it. The values espoused in this book may sound like the familiar patriotic American combination of "motherhood, the flag, and apple pie," but they are presented in all sincerity.

In a nutshell, managers need constantly to exhibit honesty, commitment, and susceptibility to reason. And while the management role is a very serious one, work should also be fun, so the manager needs to display a real sense of humor too. But to assure that the baton of leadership can be passed successfully to the next generation, the manager needs to mentor his or her employees and to encourage them to take risk wherever appropriate. Otherwise, the knowledge which he or she has gained will be lost with the manager's departure from the workplace.

Index of Topics

The topics listed below have potential to be included in a revised edition:

Build Up Old Debts For When You Need Them

Can You Work Yourself Out of a Job?

Coach Creativity

How Far Ahead Should You Look?

If You Play Well, You Tend to Win

The Horsefly Effect

Perseverance vs. Patience

Train Your Employees and Then Empower Them

What Goes Around Comes Around

Reader participation could also be fun, as well as providing interesting upgrades. If you would like to suggest a topic for inclusion, just send the topic title, a brief description, and your name, address, and phone number to the address below.

Also, additional copies of this book can be ordered directly by enclosing a check or money order for $11.95 plus $2.00 for the first book and $1.00 for each additional book for shipping and handling.

Write:
    Managing Strategically
    101 Creative Tips
    Carrot/Stick Press
    2373 N.W. 185th, #303
    Hillsboro, OR 97124

Fax:
    Managing Strategically
    101 Creative Tips
    Carrot/Stick Press
    (503) 690-0744